Books by Joe Fisher

The Case for Reincarnation
Predictions
Toronto
Skin Dive

DR JOEL L. WHITTON PhD
and
JOE FISHER

Life Between Life

Scientific Explorations into the Void
Separating One Incarnation from the Next

GRAFTON BOOKS

A Division of the Collins Publishing Group

LONDON GLASGOW
TORONTO SYDNEY AUCKLAND

Grafton Books
A Division of the Collins Publishing Group
8 Grafton Street, London W1X 3LA

Published by Grafton Books 1987

First published in Great Britain by
Grafton Books 1986

Copyright © Joel L. Whitton and Joe Fisher 1986

ISBN 0-586-07091-5

Printed and bound in Great Britain by
Collins, Glasgow

Set in Times

To those who have journeyed beyond space and time.
Their testimony has been invaluable.

Contents

Acknowledgements

The authors would like to express their special thanks to:

Dominick Abel, for his faith in the concept;
David Blizzard, for computer counsel;
Luc E. Boudreau, for investigative insights;
Felipa Gavrilos, Russell Parnick, and other eloquent ambassadors of between-life consciousness;
David Kendall, for an exhaustive literary review of the final manuscript;
Daniel Kolos, for his knowledge of ancient Egypt;
Aube Kurtz, for encouraging the original idea;
Elise McKenna, for coordinating the collaborative process;
Reva Pomer, for criticizing early drafts of the case study chapters;
Allen Spraggett, for his assistance at the outset;
Lisa Wager, for her editorial guidance;
Michelle Whitton, for researching secondary sources.

Introduction
by Joel L. Whitton

I acknowledge that reincarnation is part of my religious tradition. My precocious exposure to, among others, Hasidism and its roots in the Gerona School and the various Kabbala, Christian Neoplatonism, the Tibetan form of Buddhism, and the mysticism of the twentieth century – best represented by Theosophy, Freemasonry, the Unity Church of Truth, and the Rosicrucian Order (AMORC) – have no doubt shaped my eclectic thought.

The evidence for reincarnation, although mostly circumstantial, is now so compelling that intellectual assent is natural. Emotional acceptance may be more measured. This evidence has been assembled by other writers and is referenced in our bibliography. The reader who wishes to pursue this background of literature will find it rewarding and comprehensive and, I hope, will arrive at the same conclusion as I have: that we've lived before in past lives and will likely live again in future lives – that our current life is but a small link in a long unbroken chain.

In this book we do not review the evidence. That is worth a book in itself and has been done before. Instead, we proceed from the assumption that reincarnation is true. We do not assume, however, that every report of a past-life memory obtained under hypnosis, or claim of a spontaneously remembered past life, is what it purports to be. The issue of proof is not simple. There are important hidden assumptions in the theory of reincarnation as well as complex psychological issues in a memory of a past life. We do not articulate these issues in this book, but believe we have addressed them and have included only those cases wherein the hypothesis of past lives is the only valid one.

It is not unusual for a physician to write a theological book. Who but a physician, who assists entry into the world, is present at death, and tends to the intervening wounds, is better qualified to offer his opinion on the meaning of life and suffering. The mysteries of life and death, of the inequalities of individuals, lead to questions that material science at present cannot answer. For a physician to write a book on reincarnation, however, is unusual. Two thirds of all adult Americans believe in life after death. A 1982 Gallup Poll showed that twenty-three per cent of Americans believe in reincarnation, but only five per cent of my psychiatric colleagues do. Despite the success of Darwin in abolishing God from Nature, of Freud in reducing the divinity of man to the need to suck on a breast, and despite the supreme achievement of the Behaviourists in extinguishing consciousness, the belief in something beyond death persists. Scarcely over one hundred years ago physicians were solid in the ranks favouring immortality. Medical education seems no longer to include the study of life.

I must address one other issue. Criticism from a

few of my psychiatric and psychological colleagues, and no doubt from others with less training in the psychological sciences, will be two-pronged: *ad homenum* and *ad captandum*. The aposiopesis of the classical psychoanalysts will proclaim, as with Richard Bucke, infantile omnipotence in the belief in the possibility of the impossible, or the longing for the lost-father object in the quest for mystical experience. Because I use psychoanalytic theory in my clinical work, I know that such interpretations are not really productive in trying to understand what someone is saying. It is likely, concerning my subjects' reports, the aesthetes will burlesque them as unanalysed self-object transitional objects masquerading as ego multiples, or at least transferential phantasms. The uninformed will simply, *ad populum*, cry fantasy.

I have decided to present this data, obtained over a period of many years, as I believe that in some measure it contributes to the understanding of man's condition. I am presenting it in this popular format in order, I hope, to reach a large number of people. It is not intended to contribute to the debate of the validity, but rather to the theosophy, of past lives. I use 'past-life therapy' as a forum, as an instrument, to study the spiritual dimensions of man.

> *Joel L. Whitton, MD, PhD Toronto,*
> *January 13, 1986*

Introduction
by Joe Fisher

Joel and I weren't always such good friends.

I first came across the name of Dr Joel Whitton while gathering material for my book, *The Case for Reincarnation*. According to my sources, he was a highly qualified psychiatrist engaged deeply, if quietly, in reincarnation research. Nobody seemed to know exactly what this research entailed, but all who were acquainted with him assured me that he was a brilliant man whose metaphysical investigations would be well worth learning about.

Expecting to swell my burgeoning files on the scientific evidence for rebirth, I was introduced to Dr Whitton one spring morning in 1982. It was hardly a meeting of minds. I produced my notebook and pen, but Dr Whitton didn't want to be quoted. Aloof and clearly unwilling to invite me into the castle keep of his research, he declared, 'I'm afraid I can't help you. I'm a respectable psychiatrist. I don't want to be a lightning rod for the hostility of the fundamentalist movement.'

My frustration was barely concealed. 'What if Charles Darwin, knowing what he knew about human evolution, had shied away from writing *The*

Origin of Species?' I protested. 'Surely you are obliged to make public the knowledge you have acquired.'

Dr Whitton smiled and said nothing.

What I didn't know then was that he fully intended to publish his findings ... in his own sweet time. But in 1982 he was still dependent on the support of the academic community for funding to pursue an array of career interests, among them the study of brain waves in children with learning disabilities. The last thing he wanted was to make public his reincarnation research so that disreputable and excitable publications could ambush his 'respectable' reputation. Already, word of his professional interest in reincarnation had leaked out to some of his colleagues, prompting one department chairman at the University of Toronto to mutter darkly at a cocktail party, 'Beware of mystics ...'

Disappointed at my failure to breach Dr Whitton's defences, I returned to my typewriter and the work at hand. There were other past-life therapists to write about, after all. But I knew I was being thwarted by one of the leading exponents in the field. The most celebrated names in California and Great Britain had spoken readily in interviews ... so why not Dr Whitton, whose office was only a short walk away from my home? He had thrown me a crumb ... a brief, published summary of one of his many cases involving hypnotic regression, a case which is now fully presented in Chapter 11 of this book. I rewrote the account and dutifully presented it as a small segment of *The Case for Reincarnation*.

In time, that book was published in more than thirty countries and I forgot about Dr Whitton until October 22, 1984, when his secretary, Elise Mc-

Kenna, telephoned me. 'Would you speak to Dr Whitton?' she asked. 'He has a project he wishes to discuss with you.'

My first reaction was to tell Dr Whitton just what he could do with his project. Curiosity, however, forbade such rashness. The next day I listened as he suggested that we collaborate on a book about the intermission between incarnations. His earlier reservations about estranging the guardians of funding and raising the ire of the fundamentalists had seemingly evaporated.

Suddenly, belatedly, I was presented with the keys to the castle keep. I accepted the challenge, intrigued by the prospect of learning more about the mysteries of the between-life state. Over the next year, Dr Whitton acted as guide and interpreter as we explored the vaults of hypnotic sessions reaching back to 1973 to find remarkable similarity between the testimony of his subjects and the longstanding assumptions of scriptural authorities. Together, we endeavoured to make sense of the evidence – ancient and modern. The result is this book, *Life Between Life*.

Joe Fisher, Toronto,
January 21, 1986

Life Between Life

1

Intimations of Immortality

'In no case is there a loss of personal
consciousness to deplore. Nor will
there ever be.'

*Erwin Schroedinger,
What Is Life?*

Life's greatest mystery is a two-pronged dilemma:
Where do we come from? And what happens to us,
if anything, after death? From the earliest times,
every religious and philosophical school and every
human being with the barest modicum of curiosity
has speculated on this central conundrum. While
there is a scarcity of hard evidence, the consensus
of humanity, both ancient and modern, is strongly
inclined towards a belief in immortality. There have
always been atheists who insist that birth is a purely
biological phenomenon and that consciousness dies
with a person's last breath. Such materialistic thinking, however, is in the minority, even in today's
world of mechanistic marvels and technological

seduction. In 1982 a Gallup Poll declared that sixty-seven per cent of Americans believe in life after death.

But the question remains: If there is life after death, what is it really like? While most people acknowledge that consciousness survives the body, the nature of post-mortem activity has eluded the understanding and sometimes even the imagination. Rather than generating images of animation and vitality, thoughts on immortality incline towards vagueness and abstraction. 'The idea of life after death is indeed a completely empty one,' noted H. H. Price, a former president of England's Society for Psychical Research, 'unless we can form ... some rough conception of what "the Other Side" might be like.' Mythology, folklore, the world religions and spiritualism have made many and various claims about the next world. But only in the last fifteen years, with the emergence of intensive near-death research, has a concordance of opinion been struck between modern medical evidence and the conjecture of the ancients.

Researchers investigating the experiences of people resuscitated after being pronounced clinically dead have accumulated fascinating data. Their findings represent spontaneous sightings by 'deathbed witnesses' of another plane of existence quite different from our own. The reports concur that, at the point of clinical death, consciousness separates from the body and is drawn through a 'tunnel' into light of indescribable brilliance and sensations of utmost joy and peace. Despite not wanting to return to earthly existence, these witnesses feel compelled to reunite their free-ranging disembodied selves with the narrow confines of their abandoned bodily vehicles. On reviving, they are quick to acknowledge self-transformation. They speak volubly of having lost their fear of death (death is described as 'a homecoming' and 'like an escape from prison') and are invariably frustrated at the insufficiency of words to describe their blissful sojourn in this other form of consciousness.

Exciting and stimulating as these accounts most certainly are, the knowledge they convey is limited, just as a foreign correspondent's communiqué would be unsatisfactory if he confined himself to reporting a nation's activities from the border. Dr Kenneth Ring, the author of *Life at Death*, voiced the incompleteness of near-death research when he wrote: 'What happens *after* the initial stages of death . . . remains an open question.'

Life Between Life addresses itself directly to this question. Based on the testimony of Dr Joel Whitton's subjects who, in hypnosis, have travelled deep into death's hinterland, this book illuminates a largely unknown area of human experience. Unknown, that is, to incarnate man. The message from deep trance is that life after death is synonymous with life before birth and that most of us have taken up residence in this other world many, many times as disembodied entities. Subconsciously, we are just as familiar with discarnate existence as we are with the Earth plane – the next world is both the state we have left behind in order to be born and the state to which we return at death. As the wheel of life revolves, birth and death happen repeatedly in the evolution of the individual. Hence the title of this volume – death is no more than the threshold of consciousness that separates one incarnation from the next. Truly there is life between lives.

Dr Whitton's subjects, whose religious backgrounds are as varied as their initial prejudices for or against reincarnation, have testified consistently that rebirth is fundamental to the evolutionary process in which we are enveloped. At death, they say, the soul leaves the body to enter a timeless, spaceless state. There, our most recent life on Earth is evaluated and the next incarnation is planned according to our karmic requirements. For example, one hypnotic subject, whose actions had contributed to his sister's suicide in a previous existence, chose to reincarnate again as her brother so that he might repay this debt.

Since the age of fourteen, Dr Whitton has displayed prescient skills as a hypnotist. For some time, he practised these skills on willing subjects at parties, making no attempt to usher anyone into a previous life. But in his early twenties a developing fascination with the idea of reincarnation caused Dr Whitton to tinker with and refine his hypnotic technique. As he amassed his medical qualifications at the University of Toronto and went on to become chief psychiatrist of the Toronto school system, he found that the co-operation of those capable of entering deep trance – roughly four to ten per cent of the population – was equally forthcoming when he instructed them to travel back beyond birth into an earlier existence. 'Go to the time you were incarnate before this life,' he would say. 'Now . . . *who* are you and *where* are you?' And the person slumbering hypnotically on his couch would proceed to recount, or even re-enact, episodes from another time, another place.

As Dr Whitton gained a more intimate understanding of the unconscious mind, he instructed his patients, while in trance, to bring traumatic past-life memories into their conscious awareness. This resulted in rapid and dramatic healing which he himself cannot fully explain. Some serious mental and physical disorders simply evaporated as terrifying and disturbing memories worked a soothing magic of liberation through self-understanding. Other patients progressively shed their illnesses and psychological problems as they made contact with an increasing number of past-life and interlife experiences. Occasionally, people contacted Dr Whitton after having traipsed in vain from one clinic to another. They would tell how the ministrations of innumerable physicians had made no appreciable improvement in conditions ranging from disabling phobias to terminal disease. Because past-life regression sometimes worked where conventional medicine had failed, Dr Whitton was dubbed the 'Lost Cause Doctor'.

There is no objective proof that those who have recovered from serious disorders through past-life regression have actually re-experienced a former incarnation. The subjects themselves are convinced of the reality of the experience and Dr Whitton, having spent nearly twenty years studying past-life therapy, is confident the subconscious mind is yielding stored-up knowledge of former incarnations. Fortunately, the spectacular therapeutic results speak for themselves. As John Langdon-Davies points out in his work *Man: Known and Unknown*, 'Medicine has one great advantage over other branches of knowledge; the only criterion of truth in medicine is that it should work.'

Once guided to another lifetime, the hypnotic subject assumes a different personality and acknowledges a different body while being aware of sharing with this other self the same basic identity. Change of sex and race is commonplace. The past-life personality can be directed to any point between its birth and death and will often discuss freely the experiences of that lifetime in a voice that reflects its age, gender, culture, language, character and placement in historical time. When the store of emotionally significant memories from that life is exhausted, Dr Whitton might decide to move his subject to an even earlier existence. The person in trance then summons up another offshoot of the core identity – another unique personality grappling with a completely different existence. Always, on returning to normal consciousness, the subjects are asked to keep a diary of their trance experiences to help them capture and retain the essence of their emotional states in previous incarnations.

In order to discover the origin of a problem, Dr Whitton may choose to analyse a patient's past-life personality. In so doing, he is employing standard psychiatric procedure in a reincarnational context. Since the development of psychoanalysis, many historical and even fictional figures have been subjected to rigorous scrutiny. Sigmund Freud himself analysed Moses and Leonardo da Vinci; Freud's biographer, Ernest Jones, analysed Hamlet; Carl Jung analysed Picasso, and even Adolf Hitler was analysed *in absentia* by a team of psychiatrists in the United States. Having adopted basic Freudian principles in his practice as a psychiatrist, Dr Whitton harbours a deep respect for the unconscious. Like Freud, he believes that nothing mental is accidental, that all thought and behaviour have antecedent causes. Unlike Freud, however, he believes these causes can reach back far beyond birth to earlier incarnations and into the state between lives.

As recently as the last century, fluids from the liver and gall bladder and the position of the uterus were still thought to be among the causative agents of temperament. Early psychological researchers such as Jean-Marchand Charcot, Pierre Janet and Freud lifted the study of the mind out of the abdominal cavity and the blood vessels and into the region of the subconscious. Repressed urges and the trials of psychosexual development were recognized as determinants of human goals, wishes and fantasies.

Psychological research continued to make new and important discoveries. However, contemporary psychology, for the most part, has been limited by its premise that all adult neurotic behaviour is motivated by childhood or adolescent experience. Carl Jung had a presentiment of the cul-de-sac in which his own profession was to find itself. In *Memories, Dreams, Reflections*, he wrote:

> Rationalism and doctrinairism are the diseases of our time; they pretend to have all the answers. But a great deal will yet be discovered which our present limited view would have ruled out as impossible. Our concepts of space and time have only approximate validity . . .

Just as the early psychologists exposed the primitivism of nineteenth-century medicine, contemporary psychological thinking has been similarly revised in the light of more recent evidence. The remarkable healing – physical and psychological – that has been achieved in recent years by past-life therapists such as Dr Morris Netherton, Dr Edith Fiore and England's Joe Keeton, to name just three of the more celebrated practitioners, has demonstrated that the subconscious is only part of a greater subliminal whole. Past-life therapy identifies the higher self that transcends lifetimes and exerts a telling influence on the way we think and behave.

Dr Whitton's study of the between-life state, which grew naturally from his hypnotic investigations of previous lives, has further enhanced our knowledge of this higher self. In carrying his subjects repeatedly into the void between incarnations, he learned that human awareness in the interlife reaches a far higher pitch than that experienced during regression either to an earlier phase of this life or to a previous life. This awareness, which goes far beyond our earthbound conception of reality, enables people to see their lives from a different perspective. In the between-life state, mundane ideas of morality are enlarged on and visionary insight is granted into the meaning and purpose of human existence. Dr Whitton has a name for this extraordinary state of perception: metaconsciousness.

So how does metaconsciousness compare with other levels of awareness? The following tentative grouping of consciousness may help to explain the transcendence of this special state. First of all, on the ground floor, there's . . .

Dissociative Consciousness: A state of being in which sleeping or waking consciousness divides into two or more streams of experience. The individual, however, is usually aware of only one stream at any given time. This category includes dreams, fantasy, *déjà vu*, multiple personality states, past life memory and out-of-body experiences. Somewhat more subtle is . . .

Affective Consciousness: The apprehension of subjective states – visual or emotional or both – that cannot always be expressed by language. Among these are love, hate and the other emotions, attitudes and perceptions, and cosmic consciousness – the oneness with the universe experienced by the mystic. Which leads to the topmost tier . . .

Metaconsciousness: A supremely paradoxical state of memory awareness in which the percipient loses all sense of personal identity by merging into existence itself only to become more intensely self-aware than ever. To experience metaconsciousness – direct memory of the interlife – is to reach beyond three-dimensional reality to learn one's reason for being and the nature of personal karmic involvement. So radically different is this other world that language cannot act as a go-between and even symbols may fail to capture its essence.

Dr Whitton has found that these three different types of consciousness can coexist. A person, for example, could be dreaming (dissociative) and experiencing a subjective feeling state (affective) while recapturing memories of the interlife (metaconsciousness). He compares the three types of consciousness to a horse, a sheep and a chicken which, despite their differences, can nevertheless eat from the same bowl.

That the quality of past-life and interlife experience has great bearing on circumstances and primary relationships in this life will become apparent in the karmic case study chapters. These chapters report upon the past lives and interlives of six of Dr Whitton's subjects, all of whom are capable of deep trance. By uncovering their reincarnational history, they were able to see the reasons for varying degrees of situational hardship and emotional difficulty. This understanding, in turn, effected great change in their lives. Occasionally, an educated guess has had to be taken as to the time or location of a given past-life personality. This is because patients submerged in trance sometimes fail to divulge information which, though vital to reincarnation investigators, is irrelevant to the person undergoing a traumatic re-experience and unnecessary to the therapeutic process. The names and sometimes the occupations of the subjects have been changed to protect their identity. Nevertheless the episodes and emotions which comprise the case studies are faithfully recorded.

Only a few years ago, Dr Morris Netherton, one of California's most respected past-life therapists, denied that anyone could ever discover anything about the between-life state. 'It is virtually impossible to prove anything about the space between lives . . .' he claimed in his book *Past Lives Therapy*. 'It is not measurable, not observable to the living.' Dr Whitton has shown that, more than being merely observable, the interlife is educational, therapeutically valuable and a potential source of enlightenment. More than thirty long-term hypnotic subjects – representing a small percentage of Dr Whitton's full caseload – can vouch for the extraordinary properties of this other world. They have travelled beyond space and time into the state called meta-consciousness; they have brought back the insights and the information which form the basis for this book's pioneering observations.

2

Our Natural Home

With one word, the ancient Tibetans evoked a precise
image of the life between life. That word is *bardo*,
which literally means the space that separates
islands, a space that is crammed with events of
great significance to the soul departing the insularity
of the body. The *Bardo Thödol*, better known to
Westerners as the *Tibetan Book of the Dead*, is an
eighth-century description of the plane of consciousness between earthly incarnations where the human
entity, having crossed the threshold of death, encounters one discarnate experience after another.
Compiled and condensed from the out-of-body journeyings of generations, the book is still recited to
the dying and the deceased in hope of steering the
liberated soul across the 'dangerous ambush' of the

bardo and away from the necessity of rebirth. The life between lives, according to the *Tibetan Book of the Dead*, lasts for a symbolic forty-nine days and ranges from blissful envelopment in 'Clear Light' to a confrontation with the Lord of Death who consults his Mirror of Karma 'wherein every good and evil act is vividly reflected'.

The Tibetan *bardo* is known in the records of other cultures by a host of different names. For example, the ancient Egyptians – who built themselves meagre houses while constructing the most lavish tombs – spoke of *amenthe*, where souls dwell in continuous pleasure until descending once more to animate a new body. The Okinawans of the South Pacific spent disembodied existence in *gusho* before returning to this dimension. Australian aborigines believed the soul resided in the earthly haunts of *Anjea* between incarnations and observed a ceremony at the birth of each child in order to ascertain from whence it came. The child was later known as having been obtained from a tree, a rock, a pool of water or some other feature of the landscape, a tradition bearing echoes of Homer's *Odyssey*, which tells how people were 'born of an oak or a rock'. The Hebrews of old envisaged a stay in *pardish*, where eventually they are given instructions for the next life and sent out, according to the *Zohar*, 'sorrowing in exile; to a place where there is no true happiness . . .'

The ancients knew what modern man is just beginning to understand; that the life between life is our natural home from which we venture forth on arduous journeys of physical embodiment. Manly P. Hall in *Death to Rebirth* compares the experience of incarnation to a diver in a diving suit leaving the light and fresh air in which he is comfortable and descending, by lifeline, to the bottom of the sea . . .

. . . the heavy diving suit is the physical body and the sea the ocean of life. At birth man assumes the diving suit, but his spirit is always connected by a line to the light above. Man descends into the depths of the sea of sorrow and mortality that he may find there the hidden treasures of wisdom, for experience and understanding are pearls of great price and to gain them man must bear all things. When the treasure has been found, or his hours of labour are over, he is drawn back into the boat again, and taking off the heavy armour breathes the fresh air and feels free once more. Wise men realize that this incident we call life is only one trip to the bottom of the sea; that we have been down many times before and must go down many times again before we find the treasure.

Many primitive tribes and lost civilizations, such as the ancient Egyptians, acknowledged the life between life by making sure their dead were well-equipped to face the new world. Useful objects such as clothing, weapons and cooking utensils were buried with the deceased as a token gesture of support in case the discarnate entity remained earthbound for a time and retained the cravings of material life. In Sumerian society, which flourished north of the Persian Gulf 3,400 years before Christ, the servants of a household were slain on the death of their master so that they might also serve him in the next life.

Plato, in the tenth book of the *Republic*, recounts the strange myth of Er the Pamphylian who came to life on a funeral pyre twelve days after being killed in battle. There, he spoke graphically of the life between lives, telling how each soul was given the opportunity of selecting the form of its next incarnation. Once this selection was made, the souls drank from the River of Forgetfulness to erase all conscious memory before re-entering a physical body. Such enforced oblivion before rebirth is a persistent theme in religious traditions ranging from Chinese Buddhism to esoteric Christianity. According to the Hebrew Kabalists, the night angel Layela invokes amnesia by giving the hovering soul a little pinch on the nose while applying light pressure to the upper lip. So it is said that we all bear the mark of the angel's finger on our lips. Scriptural and mythological writings relate other common features of the between-life state, among them a sense of timelessness, the rapturous intrusion of an overwhelmingly bright light, a panoramic review of the life just passed and the soul's judgement, which is usually attended by three wise figures.

It is likely that the Roman Catholic idea of purgatory is derived from the ancient Greek interpretation of a discarnate life between incarnations. According to Rudolf Steiner, the founder of Anthroposophy, the purgatory of the Catholic Church is a recognizable, if seriously inaccurate, picture of the initial stages of the between-life state where the soul weans itself of all desires, appetites and passions. Steiner, whose knowledge of disembodied existence was gained through clairvoyance, had much to say about the plane of consciousness between lives, insisting that 'life between death and rebirth is . . . a continuation of the life here'. To Steiner, death was simply a means of restoration and rejuvenation. 'In order to sustain consciousness and to keep it active,' he wrote, 'we have been continually destroying our corporeal sheath.' He was making the point that between-life consciousness is as vital to our immortal evolution as sleep is to our physical well-being.

Since Steiner's death in 1925, there has been a growing fascination with the secrets of discarnate awareness. The hippie culture of the 1960s represented more than mindless escapism; both the urge to 'get high' on hallucinogens and the collective embrace of Eastern mysticism were indicative of a craving for ultra-physical experience – the very essence of the between-life state. And while the flower power mentality is now an anachronism, the desire to fathom the nature and extent of the soul's journeying remains. Accordingly, in recent years there have been several quasi-scientific attempts to penetrate the mystique of the *bardo*.

The world's best-known investigator of reincarnation, Dr Ian Stevenson, has referred to the interlife as 'a topic of extraordinary curiosity all over the world'. By far the highest incidence of what Dr Stevenson has termed 'intermission memories' were found in Thailand where many subjects reported they had seen their physical bodies after death and had observed their own funeral rites. Many also described being greeted in the next world by a 'man in white' and being offered the 'fruit of forgetfulness' before rebirth. Eating this fruit erases memories of the previous life and several subjects remarked that their past-life recollections were preserved only because they had managed to evade the tempting offer.

Elsewhere, some of Stevenson's subjects claim recall of the cremation of their previous physical bodies while others remember how they were directed to the home of their future birth. One subject even maintained that he had 'flitted through the air and perched on tree tops' between his death in 1928 and his birth in 1947. A relatively common feature of Stevenson's casework is the announcing dream in which a mother-to-be, usually before conception, learns that someone she has known will be reborn to her. This dream supposedly represents direct contact with the personality's disembodied awareness and will sometimes dictate a choice of name for the child. Occasionally subjects have claimed to remember appearing to their future mothers while in a transitional state between one life and the next.

While Dr Ian Stevenson travelled the world to scrutinize claims of spontaneous prebirth recall, 'armchair' studies aiming to reach similar memories through hypnosis were being attempted back in the United States. California hypnotherapist Dr Edith Fiore reported in 1978 that some of her subjects ventured into the interim between lives to find 'pure energy and light' while others saw 'beautiful lakes, beautiful scenes, gleaming cities'. There was also mention of encounters with 'planners' or a 'board of advisers', who assisted in the choice of the next incarnation which, in some cases, was preceded by the soul 'hovering' over its mother before birth. In 1979, the results of mass hypnotic studies conducted by Dr Helen Wambach, a San Francisco clinical psychologist, indicated that most people choose to be born even though they would rather remain in 'the lightness and the love' of the between-life state. Dr Wambach's subjects told of having no gender in the place between lives and mentioned, in many cases, that they had agreed reluctantly to reincarnate after consultation with 'advisers', 'a board' or 'a group of authorities'.

Those who have reported personal observations of a life between life can be compared to the mariners of old who returned from a long voyage south with an absurd tale of the sun shining from the north. Their testimony was doubted by those back home because it was at variance with the European experience of the sun's passage and defied the reason and logic of the times. To venture into the unknown is often to savour experiences that confound contemporary wisdom.

3

Stumbling upon the Bardo

'Mistake, error, is the discipline
through which we advance.'

William Ellery Channing,
Address on The Present Age

Dr Joel Whitton's investigations of the interlife were
well-advanced but still unpublished by the time California's most celebrated exponents of hypnotic regression recorded their observations. Dr Whitton
wanted to build up a substantial body of casework
before drawing any tentative conclusions. To this
end, he would spend years carrying his patients repeatedly into the between-life state to search out and
corroborate the types of experiences that all of us
can expect to encounter upon the death of our bodies.

As this chapter will relate, the initial discovery
that led to more than a decade of research happened
as the result of a technical error. When Dr Whitton
stumbled upon the *bardo* back in 1974 at the age of
twenty-eight, it had never occurred to him that active

life goes on *between* incarnations. He was so absorbed in tracing personal continuity from one life to the next that he never paused to consider what happened to human entities when they were not inhabiting physical bodies. In those days, the main thrust of his metaphysical research lay in regressing hypnotic subjects to a series of past lives. Rather than attempting to prove the theory of reincarnation, he was exploring the venerable hypothesis according to scientific principles.

Through many hours of painstaking, hypnotic sleuthing, Dr Whitton learned how to compile personal inventories of past lives stretching across thousands of years. He discovered that, according to karmic necessity, his subjects jumped in and out of incarnation to interact with the same entities in ever-changing relationships. He saw how the trials, the successes and the failures of each life contributed to the formation of the present-day individual. Moreover, no matter how disparate the various lives in each person's reincarnational history might be, they always unfolded according to cause and effect. In other words, the actions and attitudes in one life would determine the setting and challenges of a life or lives to come.

After thousands of hours of hypnotic sessions, Dr Whitton was obliged to agree with the ancient scriptures which decreed that, in the vast majority of cases, enlightenment is a prize to be won only after a painfully slow journey of purification from body to body. Personal observation showed him that the oversoul – the inner self at work behind the various incarnate personalities – is dependent upon the purging process of rebirth for its growth and development.

Back in the fall of 1973, Dr Whitton was closing in on these far-reaching convictions. Still in the throes of his preliminary studies, he had proposed to the medical committee of the Toronto Society for Psychical Research that he undertake a long-range experiment to determine the legitimacy of hypnotic regression as a means of investigating reincarnation. A controlled study of this type was long overdue as the popularity of regressive hypnosis had far out-stripped scientific knowledge on the subject.

Reports of previous existences revisited had multi-plied since the mid-fifties following widespread pub-licity given to the memories of Colorado housewife Virginia Tighe, who spoke volubly in trance of her life as Bridey Murphy, an Irish lass from the last century. Pioneering clinical psychologists and psy-chiatrists – especially in California – were fast be-coming proficient in hypnotic regression so that they could practise the latest sensation, past-life therapy. The scientific establishment refused to give the phenomenon any serious attention, having dis-missed past-life memory as elaborate fantasy. It made no difference that Dr Ian Stevenson had published *Twenty Cases Suggestive of Reincarnation*, a volume of carefully documented case studies which traced spontaneous past-life claims – many of them from the mouths of young children – to actual fami-lies in other locations.

Popular curiosity about hypnosis and past lives produced more than fifty applications from volun-teers wishing to participate in Dr Whitton's experi-ment. After carefully appraising each candidate, he selected Paula Considine. At forty-two, Paula was stable in temperament, deeply hypnotizable and –

being unexceptional in lifestyle, tastes, behaviour and expectations – the epitome of the North American housewife. She was married to a truck driver, had two teenage sons and worked as a bookkeeper for a Toronto heating company. Her very ordinariness made her the perfect subject for such an extraordinary study. Paula neither believed nor disbelieved in reincarnation and was agreeable to the post-hypnotic suggestion – to be given for her own protection – which would obliterate from conscious memory any past-life experience she might encounter. Because this was a research study rather than a therapeutic exercise, Dr Whitton was careful to instruct Paula to remember nothing of her former lives on returning to normal consciousness. He feared that the awakening of past-life memory – which, because of the sheer volume of reincarnational experience, is bound to harbour frightful episodes of suffering and brutality – might precipitate discomfort.

Starting early in October 1973, Paula made her way across town after work every Tuesday evening to an imposing last-century mansion that served as the headquarters of the Toronto Society for Psychical Research. There, in the 'yellow room' – a guest room overlooking the garden – she would take off her shoes and lie down on the couch in readiness for Dr Whitton's hypnotic instructions. Over the next year she spent more than one hundred hours in deep trance giving coherent descriptions of a long succession of incarnations, most of them female. They included:

- Martha Paine, born on a farm in Maryland in 1822. She died from a fall on the farmhouse stairs while still a young girl.

• Margaret Campbell, a housekeeper who lived near Quebec City. She was seventeen years of age in 1707 and later married a fur trapper named Arsenault.

• Sister Augusta Cecilia – age thirty-four in 1241 – who spent most of her life working in a Portuguese orphanage near the Spanish border.

• Telma, the young sister of a tribal leader in Mongolia under Genghis Khan, whom she knew as 'Temujin'. She described her age as sixteen 'summers' at the time she was killed in battle.

Paula's inventory of lives had been traced back to an existence as a slave girl in ancient Egypt when, unpredictably, her hypnotic travelling suddenly changed course. One Tuesday evening in April 1974, as she was talking in a deep trance about Martha Paine's life on the farm, Dr Whitton remembered there were further details he wished to learn about the last days of Margaret Campbell. First he interrupted his garrulous subject. Then he told her:

'Go to the life before you were Martha . . .'

Expecting Martha's childlike voice to be exchanged for that of the elderly Canadian housekeeper, Dr Whitton waited several minutes for the familiar French-accented enunciation. But no sound, save the occasional sigh, came from Paula's mouth. Her lips moved only with a constantly shifting facial expression which indicated she was watching events unfold. But what events were these? Not knowing where she was in time, Dr Whitton was wondering where he had erred when Paula interrupted his bewilderment with a rapid flickering of her eyelids. Her lips, too, puckered repeatedly as if she were searching for words and not finding them. Then, slowly and with great difficulty, she announced in a dreamy monotone:

> *'I'm in the sky . . . I can see a farmhouse and a barn . . . It's early . . . early morning. The sun . . . is low and making, making . . . making long shadows across the burnt fields . . . stubbly fields.'*

Dr Whitton could barely believe what he was hearing. Paula wasn't supposed to be 'in the sky'. So he must have made a technical error . . . but which one? Hypnotic subjects have much in common with computer programs in that their wondrous responses rest upon the most literal commands. They must be told *exactly* what to do. Make one mistake and the show won't go on—at least, not the show anticipated by the hypnotist. Dr Whitton had told Paula . . . 'Go to the life before you were Martha.' Normally, he would have commanded, 'Go to the incarnation before you were Martha.' Clearly there was a difference between the two.

'What are you doing up in the air?' asked the puzzled hypnotist.

> *'I'm . . . waiting . . . to . . . be . . . born. I'm watching . . . watching what my mother does.'*

'Where is your mother?'

> *'She's . . . out at the pump and she's having great difficulty . . . difficulty filling the bucket . . .'*

'Why is she having difficulty?'

> *'Because my body is weighing her down . . . I want*

. . . I want to tell her to take care. For her sake and for mine . . .'

'What is your name?'

'I . . . have . . . no . . . name.'

Thoroughly confounded, Dr Whitton muttered the usual directive to ensure posthypnotic amnesia and brought his subject back to the yellow room and the twentieth century. But his mind was elsewhere. By committing the mistake of verbal imprecision, he had accidentally intruded upon an uncharted realm of human experience – the gap between incarnations. His record showed that some fifty-five years separated the death of Margaret Campbell from the birth of Martha Paine. Could it be that Paula's unconscious mind was somehow tapping into the fabled *bardo* of the ancient Tibetans?

Publicly, Dr Whitton remained unmoved. He held fast to the original guidelines of the experiment and his eventual findings, which made no mention of the hovering entity waiting to be born, were assiduously objective. 'There is no reason as yet to suspect that hypnosis will successfully carry the burden of proof of reincarnation,' stated his report in the journal of the New Horizons Research Foundation. 'The memories obtained under hypnosis from the current subject are confirmed: their origin is a mystery. Believers in reincarnation will insist that the memories are true and relate to past lives; disbelievers will insist the memories are fantasy. To disbelieve is, of course, not to disprove, and to believe is not to prove.'

Privately, behind this smokescreen of ambiguity,

Dr Whitton accepted Paula's memories as genuine recollections of former lives even as her recollection of discarnate awareness over rural Maryland left him pondering the possibility of unbodily existence. In expressing adult concerns and sentiments, Martha had shown herself to be very much alive *before* entering her own physical body. And her disembodied soul, in hovering protectively over her mother-to-be, had possessed an awareness of greater range than that of an incarnate human being. For centuries there had been occasional reports of individuals who, on regaining consciousness after being pronounced clinically 'dead', had spoken of 'seeing' their bodies prostrate on a hospital bed or, possibly, at the scene of an accident. It seemed to Dr Whitton that such testimony duplicated Paula's recall of being alive 'in the sky', the only difference being that those who described their experiences on being resuscitated were self-aware in the few seconds or minutes after 'death' instead of during the days or weeks before birth.

Rather than hasten into a fresh experimental setting to research the question of disembodied awareness, Dr Whitton began to look for clues that might suggest some ancient counterpart of the hovering soul. Turning to the *Tibetan Book of the Dead*, he found an appropriate description of the human entity in disembodied residence between incarnations . . .

> '. . . you have no physical body of flesh and blood, so whatever sounds, colours and rays of light occur, they cannot hurt you and you cannot die . . . Know this to be the *bardo* state.'

Similarly, the *Katha Upanishad* of India, which dates back to the sixth century B.C., declared:

> 'The Self . . . does not die when the body dies. Concealed in the heart of all beings lies the *atma*, the Spirit, the Self; smaller than the smallest atom, greater than the greatest spaces.'

And Plutarch, the Greek philosopher, could have been speaking directly of the hovering soul over Maryland when he averred:

> 'Every soul . . . is ordained to wander between incarnations in the region between the moon and the Earth . . .'

These references could not be said to verify between-life consciousness, but each citation gave tacit support to the idea of a life between lives, the possession of uninterrupted awareness from one life to the next. However, Dr Whitton's incentive to explore the mysteries of the *bardo* was not forthcoming until the following year, 1975, and the publication of *Life After Life*, a groundbreaking study by Dr Raymond Moody which related the experiences of people who had revived after having been pronounced clinically dead. The best-selling book, which focused on the experience of dying, made no claims for reincarnation. Yet Moody's subjects spoke of 'seeing' their bodies and being immersed in a variety of sensations which removed all fear of death. Intense feelings of love, joy and peace, the presence of an indescribably bright light, participation in a process of self-evaluation and eventual awareness of a limiting barrier or border were just some of the commonly reported phenomena. *Life After Life* was generating so much interest in the idea of the next world that Dr Whitton felt obliged to look afresh at his own research, to re-examine Paula's memory of hovering over the farm in Maryland.

The more Dr Whitton reflected upon the evidence for rebirth and discarnate awareness and the more he compared this evidence with mystical and theological insight, the sharper his curiosity became. Testimony had been obtained from previous lives and from the frontiers of death and birth but the hinterland beyond incarnation remained mysterious, seemingly impenetrable. And so, like an astrophysicist lured by the awesome mysteries of outer space, Dr Whitton was drawn to inquire into the nature and dimension of the *bardo*. In time he would become the unofficial cartographer of this no-man's-land, a seasoned explorer in the limbo world. But he set out cautiously, armed only with his hypnotic technique and one enormous question . . .

> . . . *What happens to us between earthly incarnations?*

4

Life Between Life

> 'Life between death and a new birth
> is as rich and varied as life here
> between birth and death . . .'
>
> *Rudolf Steiner*

Because language is a product of worldly experience, words tend to falter and fail in the ethereal environment of the life between life. How can the inexpressible be expressed? How can the unspeakable be spoken? In his poem 'Paracelsus', Robert Browning came close to capturing the elusive essence of the *bardo*. Pointing to its accessibility deep within each of us, he wrote:

> There is an inmost centre in us all
> Where truth abides in fulness . . . and 'to know'
> Rather consists in opening out a way
> Whence the imprisoned splendour may escape,
> Than in effecting entry for a light
> Supposed to be without.

Dr Whitton has escorted more than thirty subjects – most of them over a period of several years – into the timeless, spaceless zone of this 'imprisoned splendour'. So powerful, so ineffable is the experience that first-time visitors are rendered speechless, their faces contorting with emotions of awe and bewilderment while their lips struggle unsuccessfully to describe the magnificence of their surroundings. Later, they do their best to decipher the plethora of images and impressions. In the words of one subject:

> I've never ever felt so good. Unworldly ecstasy. Bright, bright light. I didn't have a body as on Earth. Instead, I had a shadow body, an astral body, and I wasn't walking on anything. There is no ground and no sky. No boundaries of any kind. Everything is open. There are other people there and when we want to communicate we can do so without having to listen, without having to speak . . .

This blessed state, which Dr Whitton has termed metaconsciousness, can be defined as the perception of a reality beyond any known state of existence. It is distinct from dream states, out-of-body experiences, the re-living of past lives and all other altered states of consciousness. To be metaconscious is to merge into the quintessence of existence, to surrender one's sense of identity only to become, paradoxically, more intensely self-aware than ever. To be metaconscious is to be freed from bodily constraints, to feel at one with the universe, to become a cloud within an endless cloud. And while this might suggest an atmosphere of free-floating, cottonwool emptiness, the life between life is not a fairy-tale world. Those who have tasted its richness know that they have visited the ultimate reality, the plane of consciousness from which we embark on successive trials of incarnation and to which we return at the death of the body.

Once in the between-life state, the hypnotic subjects are bombarded with all manner of meaning and drama which they must somehow decode and translate in order to come to terms with their predicament and communicate their experience. Accordingly, they draw subconsciously on universal symbols – archetypes – from the collective unconscious, so named by Carl Jung, the great psychoanalyst. Only through symbols can travellers in the *bardo* hope to understand and describe this world devoid of time or space. Those who can symbolize easily have most to say; those who have difficulty visualizing tend to remain relatively uncommunicative.

The subjects who ventured into the *bardo* did so purely on an experimental basis, expecting no reward save the knowledge that they were travelling where very few incarnate humans have been. But it wasn't long before their experiences – which ranged from perceptions of a 'judgement board' to the writing of 'karmic scripts' for the next life – were found to be of therapeutic value. While the act of re-living terrifying and disturbing memories from past lives had already worked healing magic for many, immersion in the life between life contributed hugely to their self-understanding. Through metaconsciousness, they came to learn *why* they were embroiled in the circumstances of the current incarnation. Furthermore, they realized that they themselves, while discarnate, had actively chosen the setting and involvements of their earthly existence. Parents, careers, relationships and major events contributing to joys and sorrows were seen to have been selected in advance.

Most journeys into the life between life commence with a death scene. First, Dr Whitton carries his hypnotized subject back to a previous existence, scanning the final hours of that life until the person lying on his couch is on the threshold of the *bardo*. Once in a while, he will monitor progress by asking questions such as 'Where are you now?' and 'What do you see?' Typically the subject will expire in the assumed body of his or her past-life personality and then gradually begin to relate events very similar to the accounts collected by Dr Raymond Moody, Dr Kenneth Ring, Dr Michael Sabom, Dr Maurice Rawlings and other physicians who have studied and collated near-death experiences.

The inception of metaconsciousness produces drastic change in a subject's countenance. Every frown, every grimace, every intimation of fear, anxiety and pain that had accompanied the death experience drains away to leave the face at first expressionless, then peaceful and relaxed and, finally, suffused with wonderment. The eyes may be closed but there's no mistaking that the subject is captive to enthralling visions. These visions are so engrossing that Dr Whitton usually allows his subjects several minutes to become attuned to this other reality before attempting to interrupt with his own questions and directions. When he next communicates with the person lying on his couch he is talking, not to the personality before him, but to the eternal self which has produced that temporal personality. Said one subject, an electronics engineer:

> In experiencing a past life one sees oneself as a distinct personality which engenders an emotional reaction. In the interlife there's no part of me that I can see. I'm an observer surrounded by images.

The awakening to disembodied existence is where the life between life really begins. Those who have reported 'near-death' phenomena such as the overwhelming brilliance of a blinding light and a panoramic review of the life just passed, have been granted a 'peek around the corner' into the interlife. On resuscitation, the subjects of near-death experiences often speak of having approached a border or barrier which they perceive as the frontier between life and death. Dr Whitton's subjects encounter no such restricting influence on their journeys into the next world because the transition has been completed. But they are invariably confused, once they have adjusted to the welcoming waves of ecstasy and unearthly beneficient luminescence, by the utter lack of temporal sequence and three dimensions in the *bardo*. From the earthbound perspective, there is no logic; there is no order; there is no progression – everything is happening at once!

To draw insight and understanding from perceived chaos, Dr Whitton quickly learned to ask his hypnotic subjects to isolate and describe specific events from the all-encompassing collage of simultaneity. This exercise can be likened to dipping one's hand repeatedly into a bag of marbles, retrieving one marble at a time in order to establish sequence.

Of necessity, we shall assign sequence to the life between life in delineating the various experiences reported by Dr Whitton's subjects. But it must be remembered that logical succession is found only when there is proximity to the Earth plane in the period just after death and just before birth. Let's survey the commonly reported characteristics of the life between life, bearing in mind that most hypnotic subjects relay scattered remnants rather than a comprehensive account. The following is a composite portrayal of the interlife culled from a host of experiences:

RETIRING FROM THE EARTH PLANE

The idea of death aroused the most rebellious instincts in the poet Dylan Thomas. 'Do not go gentle into that good night,' he demanded of his frail and failing father. 'Rage, rage against the dying of the light.' His feelings could hardly have been more alien to the sensibilities of Walt Whitman, who wrote beseechingly of death's inevitability with the line 'Come lovely and soothing death'. Everyone has his own idea of what death will be like but few realize that these personal attitudes, together with a person's quality of life and state of spiritual advancement, exert considerable influence on the nature of the experience itself.

The smoothest transition from the incarnate to the discarnate state is accomplished by those individuals who have spent their lives moulding an outer character in accordance with the soul's highest impulses. They rejoice over the body's disintegration and are exhilarated at the prospect of being free from encasement. A person of advanced development who has a sense of incompletion about the life just passed will feel remorse at his or her inadequacy even while longing for the opportunity to rejoin the sublimity of the *bardo* state. Less-developed personalities usually adopt one of two stances. Fearing what death may bring, they may struggle in vain to remain in the body. Or, particularly if they are in poor health, they may wish to exchange their bodily vehicles as quickly as possible for a new 'suit' and rapid re-entry into physical existence. The shock of violent death often causes the disembodied soul to linger on the earthbound plane, perhaps out of bafflement, fury, self-pity or the desire for vengeance. A university professor, who relived his murder several hundred years ago as an Indian in the American Southwest, recalled his emotional state as he was about to enter metaconsciousness:

> After being tortured, killed and mutilated by three other Indians I floated out of my body feeling very angry. I thought that had I been better trained and in better physical condition I might have been able to save my life. As I left my body I made karate-like manœuvres in the air. I wanted to have a second chance to defend myself, to hang onto my life.

The much-publicized 'tunnel' experience – an archetype of transition – is a common feature of the withdrawal from earthbound existence. Time and time again, Dr Whitton's subjects have told of 'seeing' their bodies lying beneath them before being pulled rapidly through a high, cylindrical passageway. They then discover they have left their physical bodies and cannot comfort and reassure relatives and friends who have been left behind. In most cases, however, the onset of strange and wonderful experiences soon dissipates all earthbound attachment.

The tube or tunnel appears to serve as the channel of conveyance to the afterworld. Some people are met by 'guides' while still in transit and escorted into the interlife, but most subjects tell of travelling alone and merging with a multitude of strangers at the end of the journey. Whoever eventually receives the new arrival into the *bardo* – a deceased relative or friend, a conductor, or a guide who has been watching over its 'charge' during the last life – is often seen to be carrying a torch to light the way. This torch-bearing illustrates how non-material impressions are translated into symbols. By its very nature the interlife cannot be a 'place' and it cannot have torches or any other earthly paraphernalia. Thought alone exists, thought which the subconscious transforms into an object that can be apprehended. Author Stewart C. Easton wrote that the between-life state 'is not . . . up above the sky or anywhere else. It is perhaps best thought of as a condition of being that can be imagined only by thinking away entirely everything connected with the physical or bodily world.' However, if this other dimension is to be perceived, its abstract elements must be converted into imagery using symbols either from the current life or some other incarnation.

BRILLIANT BEGINNINGS

The Egyptian Book of the Dead is an after-death handbook dating back to 1300 BC. Its original Egyptian title was *Going Forth in Light*, a title which accurately reflects the experience of transition. Blinding light, overwhelming illumination, is the predominant feature of entry into the life between life. The oceanic experience of cosmic consciousness may be an apperception of this light. No earthly bliss can compare with the unalloyed ecstasy that engulfs all who cross the threshold. Love is *everything*. All-powerful rapture obliterates fear and negativity as the soul is reabsorbed into the undifferentiated one-ness of existence.

Although these brilliant beginnings greet us over and over again at the close of successive incarnations, they are usually perceived as a complete surprise. Suddenly the blinkers are torn away and we become gloriously aware of cosmic unfoldment and our place in the universal scheme of things. The enigmas of personal continuity, the nature of immortality and the process of reincarnation fall into place sweetly and effortlessly. Said a social worker who has visited seven of her lives between incarnations:

> I feel a definite physical change in trance after passing through a previous death. My body expands and fills the entire room. Then I'm flooded with the most euphoric feelings I have ever known. These feelings are accompanied by total awareness and understanding of who I truly am, my reason for being, and my place in the universe. Everything makes sense; everything is perfectly just. It's wonderful to know that love is really in control. Coming back to normal consciousness, you

have to leave behind that all-encompassing love, that knowledge, that reassurance. When I'm at a low ebb, when life is particularly unpleasant, I almost wish for death because I know it would mean my return to a marvellous state of being. I used to be frightened of dying. Now I have no fear of death whatsoever.

Another said:

It's so bright, so beautiful, so serene. It's like going into the sun and being absorbed without any sensation of heat. You go back to the wholeness of everything. I didn't want to come back.

The nature of this joyously profound revelation varies from person to person and appears to be modulated by personal experience, consciousness and expectations. Many subjects find themselves enveloped in a brilliant vault of light which radiates sensations of blissfulness and peace. Others see shades and hues so glorious that the colours of the spectrum seem positively anaemic by comparison. Some receive illumination in the form of enlightenment directly associated with their lifelong interests. A man who had lived two lives as a mathematician received his personal *eureka!* in the form of a series of equations which he knew contained the answers sought by the world's leading physicists to explain the links between various forms of energy in the universe. A woman who had incarnated successively as a musician heard music of staggering virtuosity. 'The compositions were incredible,' she said. 'This was music that the world's greatest composers could only hope to emulate.'

Those who have preconceived ideas about the next

world are sometimes rewarded in kind. An artist who was carried back to an incarnation as a Swedish child bride relived a drowning death when the Spanish galleon on which she was sailing sank in a North Sea thunderstorm at the close of the seventeenth century. She was a devout Roman Catholic in that life and, on entering metaconsciousness, her religious expectation was thoroughly gratified with visions of cherubim and seraphim against a purple backdrop, a full-throated choir and the figure of Jesus Christ welcoming her with outstretched arms.

'I THINK, THEREFORE I AM'

On Earth, we disable our thought processes in order to approach unity with the Universe, hence meditation. But in the life between life we must *start* thinking to realize our individuality. Discarnate life proceeds unconsciously and only the act of thought in the life between life allows us to see the edges of our separate clouds within the endless cloud of existence. René Descartes' famous dictum, 'I think, therefore I am' is never more pertinent than in the between-life state. There is no experience of existence without thought.

Just how much self-consciousness is exhibited in the *bardo* appears to vary greatly from person to person. Those who are keen to proceed vigorously with their spiritual development tend to be most consciously active between incarnations. Those who show little interest in the evolutionary process are inclined to 'sleep' for the equivalent of huge tracts of earthbound time.

THE DOMAIN OF THE DISCARNATE

Home is what you make it. That is to say, the environment of the life between life is a reflection of each person's thought forms and expectations. The *Tibetan Book of the Dead* asserts repeatedly that the *bardo* dweller produces his own surroundings from the contents of his mind. Rudolf Steiner maintained that thoughts and mental images of our inner realm appear to us after death as our external world. 'After death,' he said, 'all our thoughts and mental representations appear as a mighty panorama before the soul.' Adrift in metaconsciousness, Dr Whitton's subjects report a wide variety of topography. Here's a sampling:

I see splendid palaces and the most beautiful gardens.

I'm surrounded by abstract shapes of all different sizes, some oblong, some cylindrical.

Landscapes, always landscapes, and waves lapping on the shore.

I'm walking in endless nothingness – no floor, no ceiling; no ground, no sky.

Everything is extremely beautiful. There are no material things and yet everything is there ... churches and schools and libraries and playgrounds ...

I'm not aware of being anywhere. Images appear to me out of nowhere.

One man who was carried back beyond his birth in this life found himself, at first, in a huge corrugated cave. At the end of the cave stood a wall and, lifting himself to the top, he looked back to a lush, green vision of the Earth plane. He continues:

I was conscious of having a foot in both worlds. From my vantage point I could sense the vegetation and the atmosphere of Earth. But in the other direction there was much more light and the air was rarefied. With my guide, I began walking towards this other world which appeared like a scene from the Mediterranean. It was quiet, measured, peaceful. Whitewashed buildings nestled under low hills. There was a special luminosity about the buildings, each of which had low, broad-based arches. Soft, golden light was tucked up under the arches and was shining from inside the rooms.

It appears that people are sometimes afforded the setting they have imagined or have wished for while on Earth. But fundamentalists who believe that strictly doctrinaire living will be rewarded by an audience with Jesus Christ and a pew in the kingdom of heaven are courting disappointment. Dr Whitton's subjects with narrowly religious past lives have discovered in the interlife that the complex and protracted course of personal evolution cannot be supplanted by the simplistic notion of being 'saved'. Victor Bracknell, a past-life personality of Michael Gallander, the subject of our first karmic case study (Chapter 7), was a pious seventeenth-century puritan, unshakeable in his conviction that he was doing God's will. He was equally unshakeable in his belief that he would be rewarded at death by the sight of Jesus. But the life between life brought him no Christ-like vision, no heavenly haven. Instead, he was confronted with the conflicts that had caused him, in his blindness, to inflict suffering on others.

THE *BARDO* IDENTITY

To enter metaconsciousness is to be one with the timeless oversoul which is the invisible cornerstone of the powers of the individual. Intuitive awareness of this inner self is 'the germ of metaphysical realization', as Alan Watts states in his book *The Supreme Identity*. It is difficult to imagine what it must be like to merge with the very core of one's being: the knowledge is concealed in the experience. As the *Brihadaranyaka Upanishad* so lyrically declares:

> You cannot see the seer of seeing;
> You cannot hear the hearer of hearing;
> You cannot think of the thinker of thinking;
> You cannot know the knower of knowing.
> This is your self that is within all;
> Everything else but this is perishable.

It appears that each oversoul has a name which is usually beyond the reach of human comprehension. Several of Dr Whitton's subjects have reported seeing, in trance, the name of their inner identity written in an unknown language which defies all attempts at pronunciation. Could this be, we are tempted to speculate, what the eighteenth-century Swedish mystic, Emanuel Swedenborg, described as 'the language of the angels'? One man envisaged his name inscribed on a book in the form of a symbol. He did his utmost to give voice to this symbol but, try as he may, was incapable of making the appropriate sound. It seems that he was grappling with the essential language of the mind, utterly alien to vocal expression. This language of telepathic communication is used by the host of disembodied beings who populate the *bardo*, many of whom know one another from other incarnations.

When Jesus Christ said '. . . lo, the Kingdom of God is within you,' he was probably referring to the oversoul, which contains a multiplicity of personalities that have materialized in previous existences. The trance subject is able to scan the incarnate and discarnate existences of these personalities in order to make conscious past lessons that will hasten progress towards the goal of ultimate perfection. Under hypnosis, any past-life personality can, if directed, possess greater self-awareness than it had on Earth. A previous personality might be asked: 'What is going on in your unconscious mind?' – a question that cannot be answered directly by the conscious individual.

Notwithstanding the brilliant beginnings mentioned earlier, the most recent past-life personality is consumed with emotions which have their origin in the thoughts, words and deeds of the incarnation which has just ended. The animal emotions such as anger, sensate pleasure, lust, sadness and jealousy are left behind with the physical body, except in rare instances where feeling is so intense that the departing soul is branded by its influence. The cognitive emotions – love, guilt, ecstasy, admiration, remorse, loss, dread, to name a few – are maintained in the shadow or astral body. And so, ready for evaluation, the soul must face . . .

THE BOARD OF JUDGEMENT

The belief in judgement after death pervades every religious, philosophical and mystical tradition ranging from the ancient Egyptian belief in the 'weighing of the soul' before a dread tribunal to Zoroastrian teaching that a bench of judicial spirits balances each man's fate in accordance with the quality of his life. These celestial authority figures usually appear as a triumvirate. Three relentless judges stalk Greek mythology and the idea of a divine trinity crops up in the philosophy of Lao-Tzu, is represented by the Trimurti of the Hindus, and surfaces in Christianity as the Father, Son and Holy Ghost.

While the symbols and nature of the judgement drama differ from culture to culture, the purpose of the exercise is always the same: to assess the soul's performance and to chart its future course. The common state of human imperfection has always brought a sense of great foreboding to this intimate appraisal. Hebrews 10:27 refers to 'a certain fearful expectation of judgement', while the *Song of Olaf Ostesen* from Scandinavian mythology warns 'how great the sorrow of soul . . . where souls are subject to the cosmic judgement.'

The testimony of Dr Whitton's subjects thoroughly endorses the existence of a board of judgement and enlarges considerably on the rather sparse descriptions handed down from the old world. Nearly all who ventured into metaconsciousness have found themselves appearing before a group of wise, elderly beings – usually three in number, occasionally four, and in rare instances as many as seven – perceived in a variety of guises. They can be of indeterminate identity or they may take on the appearance of mythological gods or religious masters. Said one subject:

My guide took me by the arm and led me to a room where the judges were sitting at a rectangular table. They were all dressed in loose white garments. I sensed their age and their wisdom. In their company, I felt very boyish.

The members of this etheric tribunal are highly advanced spiritually and may even have completed their cycle of earthly incarnations. Knowing intuitively everything there is to be known about the person who stands before them, their role is to assist that individual in evaluating the life that has just passed and, eventually, to make recommendations concerning the next incarnation.

If there is a private hell in the life between life it is the moment when the soul presents itself for review. This is when remorse, guilt and self-recrimination for failings in the last incarnation are vented with a visceral intensity that produces anguish and bitter tears on a scale that can be quite unsettling to witness. While incarnate, one's negative actions can be rationalized and repressed; there are always plenty of excuses available. In the interlife the emotions generated by these actions emerge raw and irreconcilable. Any emotional suffering that was inflicted on others is felt as keenly as if it were inflicted on oneself. But perhaps most distressing of all is the realization that the time for changing attitudes and rectifying mistakes is well and truly past. The door of the last life is locked and bolted, and the consequences of actions and evasions must be faced in the ultimate showdown which calls to account precisely who we are and what we stand for. The opinions of others count for nothing; at stake is our personal integrity, our inner morality.

In their emotional turmoil, the trance subjects often perceive themselves as handicapped by their own wrongdoing. A man who had murdered his lover in his past life appeared before the judgement board or the Three with his own throat slashed. A mother who had inadvertently killed her own child saw herself in chains. And a woman who could not forgive herself for an act of betrayal in her previous existence expressed her burden of guilt with classical Christian symbolism . . .

> I am on one knee holding a large cross over my right shoulder. My whole anima is convulsing with pain, remorse, sadness, guilt, mourning . . . I cannot look up at the Three for sheer shame. Yet all around me there is a glowing warmth of blue rays and peace, a peace I am unable to fathom . . .

The 'peace' that this subject, a medical secretary, felt in the presence of the judgement board is commonly experienced. The judges radiate a restorative, healing energy that abolishes any handicaps and assuages all guilt. The secretary felt the cross lift from her shoulders, the man with the injured throat was made whole again, and the woman in chains was aware of the shackles falling from her wrists and ankles. Another subject commented:

> Just to be there in front of the judges made me fearful. But I soon realized there was no need to be afraid. They radiated a benevolent type of caring and my fear left me.

Rather than confirm the self-loathing and dissatisfaction of the contrite soul, the board of judgement expresses encouragement, pointing out where the life has been positive and progressive. It's as if they are saying, 'Come on now, your life wasn't *that* bad.' To justify this more balanced viewpoint, the judges preside over . . .

THE LIFE IN REVIEW

For the purpose of self-assessment, the soul is confronted with an instantaneous panoramic flashback which contains every single detail of the last incarnation. Emanuel Swedenborg dramatized this review as the recitation from a memory book of an individual's conduct between birth and death. But the experience of Dr Whitton's subjects is that the process is more immediate and all-enveloping, an absolute reliving of the last life. Said one subject:

> It's like climbing right inside a movie of your life. Every moment from every year of your life is played back in complete sensory detail. Total, total recall. And it all happens in an instant.

The review tells the soul more about the last life than the individual alone could ever hope to realize, even with full restoration of memory. An entire world of which the individual was not aware is given expression. The larger picture is etched in vivid detail so that the soul realizes for the first time when happiness was thrown away or when thoughtlessness caused pain in another or when life-threatening danger was just around the corner.

The soul absorbs every jot of meaning from this personalized videotape and this precipitates a rigorous exercise in self-analysis. This is the soul's moment of truth and, as it proceeds, the judges tend to remain in the background. They do not, according to Dr Whitton's subjects, act in the authoritarian manner suggested by cultural tradition. Rather, they behave more like loving teachers whose aim is to encourage their student to learn and benefit from past mistakes. The board of judgement frequently initiates discussion of critical episodes in the last life, offers retrospective counsel and instils reassurance that each experience, no matter how unsavoury, promotes personal development.

The individual's hopes, friendships, ideals, aesthetic inclinations and mental processes all form part of the review. Emotionalism is kept to a minimum as the judges gently assist the soul in an objective understanding of its actions within the larger context of many lives. Only by observing karmic trends and patterns – always difficult to discern within a single lifetime – can the soul gain some measure of its progress on the long, long journey of spiritual evolution.

The past-life review is presumably extracted from the Akashic Records, which seers and occultists have long observed as the indelible impressions left upon the etheric substance of the universe by everything that has ever happened. Edgar Cayce, the great American clairvoyant, said the Akashic Records were 'to the mental world as the cinema is to the physical world'. Clairvoyants may tap into this cosmic memory, and it appears that hypnotic subjects are granted access to the same vast, non-molecular library. Whenever regression focuses on a scene, a snapshot, from a previous existence, the person under hypnosis is aware intuitively of relevant details *beyond* the confines of the snapshot. This picture-in-depth is recounted in a manner that suggests the information is being drawn from the videotape of total recall.

PLANNING THE NEXT LIFE

The most significant finding of Dr Whitton's research is the discovery that many people plan their forth-coming lives while discarnate. The knowledge of self gleaned from the review process equips the soul to make the vital decisions that will determine the form of its next incarnation. But the soul does not act alone. The decision making is heavily influenced by the members of the judgement board who, mindful of the soul's karmic debts and its need for specific lessons, give wide-ranging counsel. In the Christian tradition, Jesus Christ is seen as the only incarnate being granted the privilege of choosing his parents. Metaconscious-ness, however, shows that the option is open to all and that the choice of one's parents, in establishing the setting and direction of the lifetime to come, is im-mensely important. The ancient Tibetans were well aware of this selection procedure, the *Bardo Thödol* advising the discarnate soul: '. . . Examine where you are going to be born and choose the continent.'

The judges' recommendations are made according to what the soul needs, not what it wants. So they tend to be received with mixed feelings unless the soul happens to be fanatical about pursuing its de-velopment at any cost. Said one woman:

I am being helped to work out the next life so that I

can face whatever difficulties come my way. I don't want to take the responsibility because I feel that I don't have the strength. But I know we have to be given obstacles in order to overcome those obstacles – to become stronger, more aware, more evolved, more responsible.

The price of advancement is always challenge and difficulty – the very reason why incarnations become progressively more arduous as the soul evolves. Planning for the next life is frequently undertaken in consultation with other souls with whom bonds have been established over many lifetimes. Which is to say the choice of the time and place of birth is of paramount importance; to choose wrongly is to miss the opportunity for a productive reunion.

Group reincarnation, in which the same set of souls evolves through constantly changing relationships in different lives, recurs frequently, according to Dr Whitton's subjects. The 'karmic script' often calls for renewed involvement with people who have figured, pleasantly or unpleasantly, in previous incarnations. In the words of one who felt compelled to make compensation to others:

> There are people I didn't treat too well in my last life, and I have to go back to the Earth plane again and work off the debt. This time, if they hurt me in return, I'm going to forgive them because all I really want to do is to go back home. This is home.

It would seem that the term 'soul-mate' relates to an entity with whom one has purposefully reincarnated many times in the cause of mutual growth. But growth is just as often dependent upon re-unification with those whose company is not so exhilarating. 'Oh no – not *her* again!' groaned one subject, a high school teacher, on being told his personal evolution would best be served by being reborn to a woman he had murdered in a previous life.

In order to be placed in a suitably karmic situation, some subjects were advised to accept bodies that were defective. Indeed, bodily affliction must sometimes be accepted in the cause of higher development. One woman reported:

> I chose my mother knowing there was a high incidence of Alzheimer's disease in her family and that there was every chance that I, too, would suffer from it. But my karmic links with my mother were much more important than any genetic deficiency. There was another reason for choosing my mother. The judges told me that I should undergo the experience of being raised without a father in this life and I was aware that my parents would soon be divorced. I also knew that my choice of parents would put me in the ideal geographical location for meeting the man I was destined to marry.

Not all planning is accomplished in such specific terms. Less-developed personalities seem to require the guidance of a detailed blueprint, while more evolved souls provide themselves with only a general outline, so that they must then act more creatively in challenging situations. A man who had spent a number of incarnations in a depressive, withdrawn state appreciated that his development required exposure to the sensual and the erotic in his next incarnation. He planned only that he should become an amorous female, declining to influence forthcoming events except by his basic choice of gender and attitude. As he planned the next life, he visualized . . .

> . . . a sort of clockwork instrument into which you could insert certain parts in order for specific consequences to follow. I deduced that I was working on something that I wanted to change. And I was setting up this change by working with this machinery, making the necessary alterations to the interlife plan in order that they might transpire in my forthcoming life on Earth.

This same subject was aware of the 'amorphous forms' of beings he knew from previous incarnations. One particular individual who was to figure prominently in his next life appeared in the symbolic guise of half-rose, half-cobra. Directed to search out the meaning of this symbolism, the subject discerned that the cobra aspect of the personality had twice been responsible for his death while the rose represented qualities of love that had linked the two over several lifetimes.

Finding out about one's plan can prove to be a great disappointment. A dispatcher for a cab company, who was heavily afflicted with emotional problems and feelings of inferiority, felt destined for great things if only she could remember her interlife plan. Metaconsciousness revealed, however, that her purpose in this life was simply to learn to overcome her emotional difficulties with other people. It turned out that her grandiosity was compensating for her inferiority complex. Dismayed by what she perceived as the pedestrian nature of her karmic script, she became so despondent that anti-depressants had to be prescribed. Though painful, this exposure to personal planning ultimately enabled her to proceed with the task she had established for herself.

Those who fail repeatedly to overcome major challenges in their lives find they are urged by the judgement board to place themselves in similar situations until these challenges are met successfully. People who commit suicide are frequently seized with a feeling of dread in the interlife; they know they must return to cope with the level of difficulty that led to their premature departure from the Earth plane. One subject, a doctoral candidate in nutritional sciences, learned from past-life investigation that she had a 2,000-year history of being unable to contend with being abandoned. In this life, she grew extremely dependent on her son and almost suffered a nervous breakdown when he left home for university. Meta-consciousness revealed she had once again failed her own test and that she must keep setting up similar situations for herself until she learns to master this particular weakness.

Plans can be drastically revised even as an incarnation is proceeding. This is exemplified by a subject named Steve Logan who, as a young man, felt extremely negative towards his father and rarely visited him in the Miami nursing home where he lay seriously ill. On one occasion, however, Steve, feeling that something important was at stake, was drawn to visit his father. He arrived at the nursing home to find the old man very sick and connected to a variety of life-sustaining devices. As Steve stood, alone, at his bedside, he noticed that his father was having difficulty breathing because the respirator tube had become dislodged. This situation presented

Steve with a dilemma: he could either call a nurse to save his father's life or he could turn a blind eye and allow him to die. After a moment's reflection, he ran from the room shouting for a nurse who hastily replaced the tube.

Some years later, at the age of twenty-nine, Steve had a serious bicycle accident in a small town in Oregon. He was hit broadside by a truck and was considered very lucky to escape with a fractured femur. It wasn't until Steve was in his early forties that he was carried into metaconsciousness to learn of the connection between these two events, both of which figured in his interlife planning. He reports:

> My karmic script clearly stated that the life-or-death incident with my father was most definitely a very important test that I had set myself. If I could forgive him his transgressions against me – which appeared to extend over several lifetimes – I would not be killed in the bicycle accident. The expectation was there in the plan that because of my past conduct I would allow my father to die. But I passed the test and, after my accident, the plan was at an end! I learned that sketchy plans for future lives had been brought forward to operate in the current life.

It would seem that those who have laid plans for several lives to come are those who are firmly committed to their own evolutionary progress. These resolute entities speak of spending most of the *bardo*'s duration in study of some kind. Materialistic souls, on the other hand, tell of rushing back into a body at the first sign of the interlife, while those devoid of ambition will often fall asleep once they have appeared before the judgement board only to feel, at last, awakening pressure for the resumption of earthly embodiment.

Acquisition of knowledge in the interlife prepares the soul for its next incarnation and the opportunity to put into practice what has been learned. Only through practical application can mastery be attained. Most of Dr Whitton's subjects have found themselves hard at work in vast halls of learning equipped with libraries and seminar rooms. Doctors and lawyers, for example, have spoken of studying their respective disciplines during the interlife while others remember applying themselves to such subjects as 'the laws of the universe' and other metaphysical topics. Some people even tell of studying subjects that defy description because they have no earthly counterpart. One woman reported obliquely on her investigations to discover the path to God . . .

> We are created in God's image and the idea is that we have to become Godlike, to get back to Him. There are many higher planes and to get back to God, to reach the plane where His spirit resides, you have to drop your garment each time until your spirit is truly free. The learning process never stops . . . Sometimes we are allowed glimpses of the higher planes – each one is lighter and brighter than the one before.

The planning process tells us that much of what takes place on Earth has already been rehearsed, to a greater or lesser degree, in the between-life state. Ralph Waldo Trine, in his book *In Tune with the Infinite*, said as much back in 1897:

> Everything is first worked out in the unseen before it is manifested in the seen, in the ideal before it is realized

in the real, in the spiritual before it shows forth in the material. The realm of the unseen is the realm of cause. The realm of the seen is the realm of effect. The nature of effect is always determined and conditioned by the nature of its cause.

It is almost as if we are artists who make a rough sketch of a fresco in the between-life state. Once incarnate, we set to work on the intended masterpiece, working close up day by day to execute, in minute detail, a general idea. Eventually – at death or through metaconsciousness – we are able to step back and view the work of art. Only on returning to the life between life can we know just how faithful we have been to our objectives.

Naturally the making of the rough sketch cannot ensure the real thing will follow. A plan may have been made but it doesn't have to be implemented. So is it possible to tell as life is proceeding whether we are being true to our between-life intentions? The answer must come from within. Those who are living out their karmic scripts, or have even exceeded them, have an inner sense that life is unfolding as it should. Those who have strayed from their blueprint feel, instead, that everything is out of control. Chaos rules. Like actors hopelessly unaware of their lines as they step out into the spotlight, they are forced to extemporize as the drama of life unfolds. Yet there are also people who appear to be placed precariously between destiny and fate, between scripting their lives and taking the stage as impromptu players. They have a plan, but the plan is open to an inordinate amount of improvisation.

This was the case with a thirty-seven-year-old

woman who was lured into bushland and raped near an Indian burial site in Illinois several years ago. Before consulting Dr Whitton, she spent much time and energy deliberating as to why she had been victimized. All to no avail. Her subsequent journey into the life between life revealed that the rape was not planned. At the same time, however, her karmic script indicated that she would make herself vulnerable to a random personal tragedy that would effect great change in her life. She said:

> My plan was that I would pick a tragic event which would cause me to change my entire soul complexion during my thirties. By focusing on this event, I would search with whatever means were at my disposal to find deeper meaning in my life. This is exactly what has happened.

While at liberty to reject the judges' planning advice, the soul is ill-advised to scorn their counsel. For rejection of the recommendations means that reincarnation will take place without a ratified plan – an open invitation to a life of unproductive and unnecessary trial and hardship. To be reborn without a plan is also a matter of choice. The trouble is, with no script to follow, the soul becomes a reed shaken by the wind – a victim of fate rather than a participant in destiny. No penalty is incurred for failing to heed the Three save that of a particularly remorseful self-confrontation at the end of the life that, most probably, will have been wasted.

Occasionally a trance subject has learned that he or she has made no plan in the between-life state – knowledge that is invariably communicated to Dr Whitton in fear. Those who have recourse to a karmic script, on the other hand, respond unemotionally under hypnosis even when they describe a life plan filled with hardship. Nothing could be worse, or so it seems, than to have an open future.

COMING BACK TO EARTH

The crucial decisions have been made, and all that remains is to follow through by descending once more into incarnation. Metaconsciousness makes it very clear that whereas death is truly a homecoming, a welcome respite from strife and struggle, birth is the first day of a tough new project. And while there are those who look forward with eagerness and anticipation to the challenges of earthly existence, most view with reluctance the thought of surrendering the timeless, spaceless *bardo* for material inhibition.

Some, of course, show more reluctance than others. A man who had once used and abused young boys in ancient Greece was revulsed at having to return as a persecuted homosexual. 'Oh, fuck! Oh no, not this. Anything but this!' he screamed in trance. 'There's no way I could go into that body,' he said later. 'But I had made my choice – unwillingly – on the advice of the judgement board and I just had to go through with it. I felt *pushed*.' It appears that the act of reincarnation can be resisted for only so long. Eventually, there's an accumulation of cosmic pressure that, as this subject testified, coerces the soul to renew its development within the confines of a physical body.

Just how much time is spent out of incarnation

varies widely from person to person and from life to life. Among Dr Whitton's subjects, ten months is the shortest interval observed between lives while the longest extends for more than eight hundred years. The average between-life stay – approximately forty years – has been steadily diminishing over the past several hundred years. In the old world, when the globe changed little from century to century, there was less incentive to reincarnate than there is today. The recurring transformation of the modern world appears to entice entities ever hungry for new earthly experience to reduce their time out of incarnation – a factor that could well account for the huge rise in the global population. Several of Dr Whitton's subjects, having died during World War Two, have reincarnated in time to join the 'baby-boom' generation.

Less-developed souls who thirst for a new body, any body, won't spend long in the life between life. Nor will those who see an early opportunity arising on the earthbound plane to make karmic compensation for actions in earlier lives. Extended stays may arise from the desire to expend great effort in preparation for the next earthly existence or may stem from an apathetic attitude towards evolutionary progress, an attitude which often results in disembodied slumber until the 'wake-up call' of the next incarnation. Herodotus, the Greek historian who lived during the fifth century BC, mentions that the ancient Egyptians taught that each soul spent a 3,000-year period between incarnations. Modern hypnotherapists, however, have thoroughly revised this estimate, noting that many of their subjects have been reborn several times within the twentieth century. Seth, the famous spirit guide who communicated through the mediumship of author Jane Roberts, maintained that personal choice unfailingly determines the *bardo*'s duration. He said, 'It is always up to the individual. The answers are within yourself then, as the answers are within you now.'

Before entering the Earth plane, the entity passes through an etheric barrier which serves to lower the vibrations of its consciousness. Beyond this barrier – symbolized by the classical River of Forgetfulness – memory of the *bardo*'s magnificence dissolves. This amnesia is invaluable in that it prevents endless pining and homesickness for the grandeur that has been left behind and allows the individual to embark on the new life unhindered by confusing echoes of past deeds and misdeeds. Equally importantly, knowledge of any plan the soul may have made for the forthcoming life is necessarily subjugated. Just as it is pointless for a student to be furnished with answers before sitting down to write an examination, so the test of life requires that certain information is temporarily withheld from the conscious mind.

First awareness of actually being in the body is reported at times ranging from several months before birth to just after emerging from the womb. Many of Dr Whitton's subjects have mentioned 'hovering' over the mother, encouraging her in choices of food and music, discouraging smoking and the drinking of alcohol, and generally directing behaviour that will enhance their mutual welfare. In several cases, a name was communicated for the embryonic child.

Does the soul enter the body gradually or suddenly, long before birth, at the time of birth, or after the baby has been born? Or can there be great variability from person to person? These are vital questions for which, as yet, no definite answer has emerged from the mass of conflicting evidence. The issue is confused by the presence of two types of memory – brain memory and soul memory. Because the brain memory is functioning within three months of conception, it is difficult to know whether subjects under hypnosis are relaying messages from the central nervous system or from the presence of the eternal 'I'. This uncertainty, while relevant to the hotly debated question of abortion, offers no solutions. We would say only that if the soul is within the body when an abortion is performed, the killing of the foetus can be equated with the act of murder; if not, the abortionist is doing nothing more pernicious than removing a piece of bodily tissue.

The abortion issue is further complicated by the belief of the Druses of Lebanon that reincarnation takes place without a *bardo*, that a new being is born at the death of its former body. The Jains of India, in similarly dispensing with the between-life state, say that a new being is conceived when its previous body dies. Edgar Cayce's data suggests that the soul can enter the body shortly before birth, shortly after birth or at the moment of birth. In general, Dr Whitton's subjects support Cayce's clairvoyant assertions in reporting birth experiences such as this one:

> I was in the delivery room watching my mother and the doctors standing around her. White light surrounded everything that was going on and I was one with this light. Then I heard the doctors say, 'It's coming!' and I knew that I had to merge with my new body. I was very reluctant to enter this life. It felt so wonderful being a part of the light.

As the new life progresses, the life between life may as well never have existed. The child develops a central identity which usually makes the assumption that itself and the temporal physical environment comprise the only reality. As language is developed, possible inklings of the original and more refined state of existence are relegated to notions of 'unreality', dismissed as vague, abstract and highly speculative.

When people regain normal consciousness after deep-trance travelling in the interlife, they are frequently shocked, disorientated and dismayed. Like tiny tots who have been snatched from the candy store of their dreams, Dr Whitton's subjects ache to return to the land of perfect understanding, the land where the meaning of life is self-explanatory and the soul and its immortal purpose are as diaphanous as glass. 'You've woken me up in an unreal world,' one subject complained. 'Now I know where the true reality lies.' Even a glimpse of the 'true reality' brings the knowledge that the *bardo* experience is bound to recur, if only because one is contained in a bodily vehicle that must perish. This, in turn, removes all fear of death. In the words of one subject: 'Now I am able to really look forward to death knowing that it is something very beautiful.'

While virtually every traveller in the life between life retains a sense of this marvellous other world on waking, few are able to elucidate their memories to their own self-satisfaction despite having given relatively cogent accounts while in trance. 'It's so *different*,' they will say, fumbling for words. 'I can't explain it exactly,' said one woman. 'But I now know the reasons, the whys and the wherefores, for my own life.' Part of the difficulty in interpretation lies with the uniqueness of metaconsciousness. Human beings will try to describe strange happenings in terms of what they already know, but there is nothing on Earth which can compare with the inter-life. Even symbols may fail to grasp the nature and meaning of the experience.

Then again, people may censor their recall. 'I can withhold information, but I cannot lie,' one subject noted. There's a strong inclination to suppress any powerfully negative emotions. And self-imposed am-nesia will surely follow wherever the soul decides that conscious knowledge of approaching events will impair karmic unfoldment. Several times, hypnotic subjects have glimpsed future events in their lives and then asked Dr Whitton to erase the memory from their consciousness. 'Please do not let me remember this when I wake,' they have requested. 'I might be tempted to tamper with my karma.' Others have jumped out of trance as they are relating the circum-stances of their future only to find themselves unable to remember anything that has transpired.

Nevertheless some subjects have felt at liberty to scan their karmic scripts, bring the knowledge into conscious awareness and predict future happenings in their lives. Whenever these predictions were sufficiently short-term to allow for verification, they proved to be accurate. But more frequently subjects were granted a hint – and no more than a hint – of what lay in store. In August 1984, a heavy equipment operator learned from metaconsciousness that he was to be waylaid by 'something extremely bad' in the fall of 1985. He had no idea what this ominous event might be and he knew that he must not try to discover its precise nature in case he felt inclined to take steps of avoidance. 'Whatever this is,' he said, 'I know I must go through it for the sake of my development.' On September 15, 1985, a sudden, severe asthmatic attack landed him in hospital for two weeks, the first four days of which were spent in an intensive care unit.

All who return from the *bardo* have a different tale to tell. While similar in theme, their accounts vary as to the degree of light or enlightenment at the threshold, the appearance of the judgement board (some people don't visualize the Three but merely sense the recommendations of a higher authority), the extent to which the karmic script may be examined, and many other details. But in one fundamental aspect the privileged few who have visited the interlife receive the same unrelenting message: *We are thoroughly responsible for who we are and the circumstances in which we find ourselves. We are the ones who do the choosing.*

Total self-responsibility may be perceived as freedom on the edge of a razor, but the terror is mitigated by the knowledge that we are all partaking in an awesome evolutionary process that invests each thought, word and deed with meaning and purpose. Having glimpsed how each succeeding incarnation is elected on the basis of one's past, travellers in the interlife are bound to return to this life with a heightened awareness of their responsibilities. But they also retain an acute appreciation of the moral sensitivity at work in the macrocosm, a sensitivity which pervades their own incredibly complex voyaging in and out of life incarnate. Exposure to this deeper reality, this larger harmony, promises nothing but liberation through understanding. As Cicero observed in *De Legibus* after peering into the world beyond, 'We at last possess reasons why we should live; and we are not only eager to live, but we cherish a better hope in death.'

5

The Shuttle of Rebirth:
Our Journey So Far . . .

'We all return; it is this certainty that
gives meaning to life . . .'

Gustav Mahler

Take away reincarnation and the interlife is no more
conceivable than a river without banks or sleep without wakefulness. The very nature of the *bardo* requires that each discarnate experience be flanked by
earthly existences. Hence the need for the shuttle of
rebirth which carries us into physical embodiment
and returns us, at death, to the non-material plane
of consciousness between lives.

The hypothesis that we are impelled to return to
Earth, again and again, in different bodily vehicles is
well supported by cultural tradition, religious doctrine and scientific research. But all the eloquence
and evidence in the world won't make the idea any
more palatable to the individual who chooses to
believe otherwise. Acceptance of rebirth goes hand

in hand with exploration of our true spiritual natures, and scant encouragement exists for such scrutiny of the self in modern society. Humanity's spiritual component has been neglected, even scorned, by a Western civilization weaned on dogmatic conditioning. Charles Darwin's *The Origin of Species*, so revolutionary during the latter half of the last century, no more than hinted at the vastness of human evolution. Darwin spoke only of physical unfoldment. He left untouched the bigger, more complex theme of spiritual progression which carries mankind from lifetime to lifetime through manifold shifts of consciousness.

In a world predominated by materialism, 'the instinct of the race', as Henry David Thoreau described reincarnation, is usually smothered at a very early age. Nevertheless in 1982 a George Gallup poll indicated that twenty-three per cent of all Americans believed in rebirth (as mentioned before, sixty-seven per cent believe in life after death) while, three years earlier, a London *Sunday Telegraph* poll reported that the belief was held by twenty-eight per cent of the British population – an increase of ten per cent in ten years. Tin buttons for sale in the British Isles wittily declaim: *Reincarnation Is Making A Comeback*. Not that there's anything radical about the trend. Rebirth has always been espoused by the wisest of spiritual and philosophical sages – from Plato to Jesus Christ – and, historically, has figured prominently in the annals of human thought and behaviour.

Let's start with our prehistoric ancestors. Long, long ago the scattered tribes of the world accepted reincarnation as a law of life. Death signified a return to Mother Earth from whose womb the individual would arise once more. The skeletons of Neanderthal Man – dating roughly between 200,000 BC and 75,000 BC – have been found pressed into the foetal position, as if in expectation of the next incarnation. Shamanic belief, which reaches back into the Upper Palaeolithic period between 15,000 and 25,000 years ago, held that humans and animals were reborn from their very bones where the essential life force was thought to reside. In some North American Indian tribes, anyone who aspired to be a shaman was required to remember his ten most recent deaths. Tribal memory, ancient myth and fable, religious belief and classical wisdom all bear witness to the conviction that repeated incarnations are as essential for spiritual evolution as the succession of years is to physical development. Rebirth has always been seen as the mechanics, the framework, of immortality: the means by which perfect enlightenment can eventually be attained.

Between lives we are at one with our celestial heritage. When we return to Earth to resume forging our destinies in the heat of physical experience, our familiarity with the wellspring is temporarily forgotten. The repressed knowledge of the interlife mutates into faith and belief. These, in turn, become religion: a yearning and striving for the sublimity that has been left behind. Reincarnational teaching wistfully pervades the most venerable religious scriptures. In Buddhist texts the transition from body to body is compared to the flame that passes from candle to candle and the soul is portrayed as shaping bodies to its needs as the goldsmith fashions designs in gilt. Ancient scripture abounds with references to the wheel of rebirth which swings human beings, fastened by the chains of karma, through cycles of existence. Karma – the subject of the next chapter – is the name given to the factor of self-determination which regulates conditions for the series of incarnations. Literally meaning 'action', karma represents the complex interplay of cause and effect in life after life while its demands, as we shall see in the case study chapters, are felt keenly in the between-life state. St Paul said in Galatians 6:7, 'Whatsoever a man soweth, that shall he also reap.' This is karma's impersonal accountancy at work; everything an individual thinks and does acts upon the universe to create its own reaction.

Because of Hindu and Buddhist teaching, well over one billion Asiatics accept that they must undergo round after round of birth and death. Their hope is that, through selflessness, compassion and the pursuit of knowledge, the dread bondage to the wheel can be speedily exchanged for *moksha* or deliverance. But they also recognize that in most cases human failings dictate otherwise, that karmic workloads and the desire for the sensuous pleasures of terrestrial life ensure a painfully slow journey of purification from body to body. Gautama Buddha, who is said to have lived 550 previous lives during more than 25,000 years, stressed that attachment to earthly existence confined human beings to the treadmill of rebirth.

Long before Buddha was born, the ancient Greeks and Egyptians had developed a sophisticated awareness of the process of reincarnation. Egyptian writings tell how the god Osiris, who personified esoteric knowledge, was driven to Egypt from India in the form of a spotted bull. Greek texts referred, in phraseology that foreshadowed classical Indian belief, to 'the sorrowful weary wheel'. Meanwhile, the ancient inhabitants of northern Europe were so confident of rebirth that they wept in commiseration at the birth of a child and greeted death with rejoicing. It is said that the Druids, with even greater conviction, accepted that if borrowed money could not be repaid in this life, the debt could be made good in the next incarnation! Indeed, the old world was so imbued with this way of thinking that the word 'education' originally meant 'to draw from that which already was known'. Enlarging on this theme in his Theory of Reminiscence, Plato declared, 'Knowledge easily acquired is that which the enduring self had in an earlier life, so that it flows back easily.' Cicero, the great Roman orator and philosopher, concurred by maintaining that the speed with which children grasp innumerable facts is 'a strong proof of men knowing most things before birth'. Child prodigies certainly provide strong circumstantial evidence for the assertion that talent is not necessarily developed in the life at hand and might have its origins in previous existences.

Even though orthodox Christianity, Judaism and Islam deny reincarnation, each of these great schools of religious thought have accommodated factions which have argued vociferously in its favour. Contrary to popular belief, rebirth was widely accepted by many early Christians, notably by Origen, who has been hailed by the *Encyclopaedia Britannica* as 'the most prominent of the church fathers with the possible exception of Augustine'. Clearly, St Augustine agonized over the prospect of multiple existences. 'Say, Lord, to me . . .' he wrote, 'say, did my infancy succeed another age of mine that died before it?' Perhaps he did not know, as many modern Christians do not know, that Jesus Christ testifies on reincarnation's behalf both in the Bible and, more explicitly, in the Gnostic scriptures. The Gnostic gospel *Pistis Sophia* quotes Jesus as saying that 'souls are poured from one into another of different bodies of the world'.

Not until the fourth century, when Christianity evolved from harried bands of secret worshippers to an institution ripe for political manipulation, did opposition develop to reincarnation in Christian theology. The new Church-State alliance, aiming for the cultivated dependence of the masses, felt threatened by those who believed in rebirth because such Christians tended to be self-reliant, free-thinking individuals whose subservience could not be guaranteed. Neither to be induced by promises of heavenly bliss nor intimidated by threats of hellfire, they were branded as heretics (the word 'heretic' means, at root, nothing more pernicious than one who is 'able to choose'). Nevertheless, there was no official edict condemning the doctrine of reincarnation across the Roman empire until the year AD 553 when the Emperor Justinian issued formal ecclesiastical curses against the 'monstrous restoration' of rebirth. This censure was followed by persecution of all who refused to surrender their convictions. Resistance, however, was so tenacious – particularly by rebel Christians called the Cathars – that not until the thirteenth century did the church's campaign of terror and slaughter effectively rout re-incarnational thinking in the West. But there was no extinguishing the pilot light. Secret mystical groups such as the alchemists and the Rosicrucians made sure the belief was smuggled forward to modern times.

The loosening of the ecclesiastical straitjacket began in earnest in the Renaissance with a spontaneous exaltation of individuality. During the Age of Enlightenment that followed, many of the great minds of Europe adopted the idea that having many lives vested an otherwise unfair and pointless existence with justice, meaning and purpose. 'After all,' noted Voltaire, 'it is no more surprising to be born twice than it is to be born once.' Such heady reasoning, however, failed to sway the masses. Most people were steeped in fundamentalist concepts that preached the stark post-mortem alternative of either paradise or eternal damnation. Time moved on, but little changed. The strict Victorian mentality and the nuts and bolts excitement of the industrial revolution were hardly conducive to a resurgence of interest in reincarnation. And yet that era's implicit denial of the presence of higher consciousness invited the challenge to materialism that appeared in the form of the Theosophical movement and the expansion of the Rosicrucian Order.

During the second half of the last century, the Theosophists swam gamely against the prevailing current by importing, for westerners' perusal and edification, much of what has come to be known as The Wisdom of the East. Their cause had limited appeal and was soon overwhelmed by the emergence of thinkers who denied the existence of a spiritual world – men such as Karl Marx, Sigmund Freud and Bertrand Russell. Simply by quoting and expounding upon Eastern mystical writings, the Theosophists could not expect the idea of rebirth to survive in the brash intellectual climate of the twentieth century. Against a backdrop of developing technological grandeur, the pressure was on to confirm or deny, empirically, the reality of the enigma called reincarnation. During the 1890s, a Frenchman by the name of Colonel Albert de Rochas had taken the first hesitant steps towards a scientific methodology. Imitating the style of Franz Anton Mesmer, the Austrian physician who gave his name to hypnosis or 'mesmerism', de Rochas swept his subjects back beyond birth into a succession of 'past lives'. The veil had been lifted on a new dimension of human experience, raising at once the question that is still being asked today: Does past-life testimony from the trance state truly reflect a previous existence? Because he failed to prove the historical veracity of his subjects' lives – even though they gave plausible testimony, mentioning places and families that were often known to have existed – de Rochas was left brooding upon 'the darkness in which all observers have to struggle at the beginning of every new science'.

For years after de Rochas' tentative explorations, psychiatrists and psychologists cited mental derangement as the reason for their patients' occasional spontaneous recall of other lives. Rival explanations such as extrasensory perception, spirit possession, and cryptomnesia – the welling up of forgotten memory originating in the present life – are still offered to dismiss claims of past-life experience. The difficulty is that even when a past life is historically verified, nobody can *prove* that the person with all the emotion and information was once the individual he or she claims to have been. Like the concepts of heaven and hell, reincarnation is a metaphysical proposition and will be constrained neither by earthbound 'reality' nor judged by our earthly limitations. Proof must yield to perception.

The earliest experiments in hypnotic regression caused quite a stir in professional circles, but it was left to amateur hypnotist Morey Bernstein to capture the public imagination, in 1954, with Bridey Murphy – a persona produced by Colorado housewife Virginia Tighe whenever she was hypnotized by candle flame. Her vivid and detailed accounting of life as Bridey in nineteenth-century Ireland made headlines across the western world provoking millions of conversations about rebirth and a spate of *Come As You Were* parties. In the late 1920s, the work of the great American seer, Edgar Cayce, had attracted a smaller, but committed, audience to the idea of reincarnation. Cayce, a devout Presbyterian, initially rejected the idea of rebirth. But on August 10, 1923, he emerged from a self-hypnotic trance to be told of his declaration that people are reborn in different bodies. Fearing, at first, that his subconscious faculties had been commandeered by the devil, he soon accepted his own testimony that karmic patterns are woven into personal histories spanning thousands of years. Cayce came to understand that reincarnation does not impugn the teachings of Jesus Christ. He proceeded to give 2,500 'life' readings over the next twenty-one years. Many times he traced present infirmity to deeds – or lack of deeds – in past lives. This led him to reject the conventional conception of heredity. When someone asked 'From which side of my family do I inherit most?' he retorted, 'You have inherited most from yourself, not from your family! The family is only a river through which the soul flows.'

Edgar Cayce's voice was heard at a time when the world was beginning to ripple with tremors of spiritual revitalization. After centuries of mutual alienation, science and mysticism edged closer together as the interdependence of mind and body, matter and spirit was more readily acknowledged. Albert Einstein's theories of relativity showed that classical Newtonian physics had failed to penetrate the true nature of time, space and motion. The so-called 'new physics' that followed made the discovery that subatomic particles are constantly dying and being reborn, that every subatomic interaction consists of the annihilation of the original particles and the creation of new ones. In other words, a microscopic form of rebirth underlies everything in the physical world. The same principle seemed to be at work in the most macroscopic of arenas as astro-physicists proposed that the universe itself is forever dying in order to be reborn. This all-embracing vision of death and rebirth has long been symbolized by Shiva, the four-armed Hindu god of creation and destruction. It is also implicit in the ancient Chinese *Tao*, whose relentless cycles of coming and going signify the very nature of the life process.

While physicists probed and tested the cosmic pulse, the exponents of hypnotic regression continued to explore the foggy borderland of the human unconscious. The most notable successors to the pioneering Colonel de Rochas were Sweden's John Björkhem and Dr Alexander Cannon, an Englishman awarded degrees by nine European universities. Between them, they dredged up vast amounts of past-life material. Although Dr Cannon regressed 1,382 volunteers to time periods as far back as several thousand years before Christ, he only accepted their testimony under duress. In 1950, Dr Cannon wrote in *The Power Within*:

> For years the theory of reincarnation was a nightmare to me and I did my best to disprove it and even argued with my trance subjects to the effect that they were talking nonsense. Yet as the years went by one subject after another told me the same story in spite of different and various beliefs. Now well over a thousand cases have been so investigated and I have to admit that there is such a thing as reincarnation.

Dr Cannon, who went on to claim that the work of psychoanalyst Sigmund Freud had been 'outflanked by reincarnation', specialized in tracing the origins of complexes and fears to traumatic incidents in past lives. Dr Whitton's casework has built upon his legacy. Cannon was the trailblazer for a profession which, in the 1970s and 1980s, has been responsible for healing hundreds of thousands of people. Past-life therapy, at its best, demands of its practitioners a high degree of patience, intuition and technical virtuosity. Many hours may have to be spent probing a subject's succession of previous existences in order to locate the source of the aggravation in another time, another place, another body. But the healing of both physical and psychological disorders is often rapid and dramatic once pertinent information has been wrested from the subconscious mind.

No one can state with certainty how or why the remedial process works, but it appears that the very act of confronting and accepting negativity long trapped in the psyche provokes some alchemy of liberation. The beneficiaries of past-life therapy range from truck drivers to movie stars. They find themselves identifying emotionally with their encountered personalities whether the trance state allows them to enter their former bodies or just to observe their transformed selves from afar. Practically all past-life therapists are convinced that their subjects actually re-experience their own previous existences. Said Dr Edith Fiore, a clinical psychologist from Saratoga, California, 'If someone's phobia is eliminated instantly and permanently by the remembrance of an event from the past, it seems to make logical sense that that event must have happened.'

Dr Helen Wambach, another California-based clinical psychologist, set out several years ago to prove or disprove the theory of reincarnation. Her research relied upon statistical studies of hundreds of hypnotized subjects who, regardless of their sex in the current lifetime, divided strictly according to biological fact by recording 50.6 per cent male and 49.4 per cent female lives when regressed to time periods as far back as 2000 BC. Even though these subjects were primarily white, middle-class Americans, their remembered incarnations also accurately reflected race, class and population distribution in the historical world. Moreover, their reports of clothing, footwear and eating utensils used across the centuries agreed with historical fact. Dr Wambach's studies left her 'knowing', rather than believing in, the process of reincarnation. She explained, 'If you are sitting in a tent on the side of the road and 1,000 people walk past telling you they have crossed a bridge in Pennsylvania, you are convinced of the existence of that bridge in Pennsylvania.'

Incontrovertible evidence for rebirth is, as we have stated, a practical impossibility because it cannot be proven that a person with memories of a previous existence actually *was* that remembered individual. This dilemma calls to mind the words of American psychologist William James, who said, 'If you wish to upset the law that all crows are black, you must not seek to show that no crows are: it is enough if you prove a single crow to be white.' For more than a quarter of a century, two investigators of past-life memory – Dr Ian Stevenson and Hemendra Banerjee – have done everything in their power to produce that lone white crow. So far the bleached bird has stubbornly refused to make an appearance. Undaunted, Stevenson and Banerjee have concentrated their efforts in testing and collating the spontaneous past-life utterances of hundreds of young children living in many different parts of the world. Time and time again, they have matched the claims of these youngsters with real-life historical personalities and locations. And so the casebooks of these two dedicated investigators show that while white crows cannot be produced for public inspection, their existence is not easily dismissed.

Dr Stevenson, who has more than 2,000 child cases filed on computer at the Department of Parapsychology at the University of Virginia, has said that 'a rational man can, if he wants now, believe in reincarnation on the basis of evidence rather than simply on the basis of religious doctrine or cultural tradition'. At the same time, he is careful to point out, 'Neither any single case nor all of the investigated cases together offer anything like a proof of reincarnation. They provide instead a body of evidence suggestive of reincarnation that appears to be accumulating in amount and quality.' Indicative of this accumulation are the more than two hundred birthmarks Stevenson has examined on children who claim to have been killed by bullets and bladed weapons that pierced the corresponding parts of their anatomies in a previous life. In seventeen such cases, he has obtained medical documents such as hospital records or autopsy reports that establish the past-life individual was put to death in the way described.

Hemendra Banerjee, who founded the Indian Institute of Parapsychology in 1957 and has been living in the United States since 1970, became convinced of the reality of reincarnation by observing children's spontaneous emotional recognition of past-life relatives and friends. In this context, children are credible witnesses; the testimony of these youngsters – usually aged between two and five – has yet to be contaminated by cultural prejudice or overwhelmed by the pressing demands of worldly experience. Usually a violent act has put an end to the lives that they remember. It can only be supposed that this violence produced an emotional reaction strong enough to pierce the natural amnesia that separates them from their former incarnations.

Toddlers who remember past lives will mutter such phrases as 'When I was big' and will perhaps complain about not being the same sex as before. They might yearn for the lost companionship of a relative or friend and hanker for the food, clothing and life-style – even the alcohol, drugs or tobacco – of a former existence. But there's little likelihood they will be heard sympathetically, even though they may be crying out in protest at the trauma that launched them precipitously into the interlife. Whatever these guileless witnesses say is too often ignored or discouraged by western parents while, in the East, because of a superstition that those who remember a previous existence are fated to die young, it is not uncommon for parents to dam the flow of past-life recall by filling their child's mouth with dirt or soap.

Frequently the question is asked: 'If reincarnation exists, why can't we all remember our past lives?' Mohandas K. Gandhi, the great Indian philosopher and apostle of non-violence, attributed a certain benevolence to the cosmic process when he replied, 'It is nature's kindness that we do not remember past births. Life would be a burden if we carried such a tremendous load of memories.' Yet it is possible to break through this amnesia either with the aid of hypnosis or by activating 'far memory' through practised and purposeful meditative techniques. One of the most popular arguments against reincarnation maintains that all past-life memory is really genetic in origin, that the hereditary line accounts not only for physical resemblance and a person's strengths, weaknesses and predispositions but also for recall beyond birth which is, supposedly, coded in the DNA molecules. The evidence of hypnotic regression promptly dismisses this contention. In trance, whites have described existences as Negro slaves and many subjects have talked about being incarnate during their parents' lifetimes. In any case there simply is not enough DNA to code even one life's memories, let alone several lifetimes.

The evidence under review suggests that the shuttle of rebirth is an evolutionary requirement which grants us the means to learn from experience and, through learning, to realize our vast potential. One life is simply not enough. The world's leading expert on death and dying, Dr Elizabeth Kübler-Ross, has written that it is 'practically impossible' to fulfil our destiny in one lifetime. California past-life therapist Dr Morris Netherton argues, 'It took nature ten million years to build the Grand Canyon. I can't believe it takes just seventy or eighty years to build a man's soul.' Dr Whitton's case studies confirm that we constantly exchange the interlife for incarnate existence with the expressed intention of expending greater effort to refine our innermost being. There is no substitute for personal experience and only by choosing different bodies, according to our needs, can we learn from a multitude of perspectives.

On Earth, immersion in lives of war, disease, crime, affluence, motherhood, confinement, fame, guilt, hunger, disillusionment and much, much more serves to spur the growth of knowledge, wisdom, compassion and all else that prepares us for the elevated state beyond the pull of earthly incarnation. To say that perfection takes a long, long time would be an understatement. The journey would be intolerable without the constant change of scene and sustenance that comes from cycling in and out of incarnation. Earth life is not only difficult, it's myopic – we rarely see beyond the desires and imperfections of our physical frames and the flux of circumstances into which we cast ourselves. Yet at death we regain the grander vision of the disembodied state in order to rest, evaluate, and acquire further learning in readiness for the next round of rebirth. Then, having filled our sights with the life to come, we plunge once more into the crucible of earthly existence where deeds determine destiny.

6

The Cosmic Classroom

'We choose our joys and sorrows long
before we experience them.'

Kahlil Gibran,
Sand and Foam

Momentum is essential to personal evolution. Without momentum, there would be no learning; there would be nothing to propel the soul through the myriad of experiences that arise in the course of its journeyings from incarnation to incarnation. This thrust, this impetus, is entirely self-generated and goes by a Sanskrit word which has lodged itself firmly in the English language: 'karma'.

Karma is that which individuals have set in motion for themselves from lifetime to lifetime by their motivations, attitudes and behaviour. Acceptance of karma dismisses the idea that humans are mere pawns in a cosmic chess game. To accept karma is to acknowledge that the world is an arena of natural justice: there can be no unfairness, inequality and misfortune if all conditions arise as a direct result of past conduct. Karma weds self-responsibility to the law of cause and effect; one's actions from life to life give shape and substance to personal continuity and personal destiny. Said Gautama Buddha, 'If you want to know the past, look at your present life. If you want to know the future, look at your present.'

Traditionally defined, karma is a system of retributive justice that perpetuates rebirth and determines the form and setting of each succeeding incarnation. The ancients taught that karma is discharged according to 'an eye for an eye' philosophy which maintains that, sooner or later, people will experience for themselves precisely the joys and sorrows they create for others. But, according to Dr Whitton's subjects, life doesn't *have* to work out that way. Those who have visited the *bardo* insist that karma is, essentially, learning. It is the principle at work in all things that makes possible the development of the soul. To learn is vital but the way in which the learning is accomplished — whether through violent exchange, laborious application or sophisticated insight — is relatively unimportant. Certainly, service is fundamental to the process, the statement 'When you help another, you help yourself' emerging as the most basic tenet of karmic law. 'Love one another,' counselled Jesus Christ. There is no better advice for those who seek the most direct way to reduce karmic accumulation.

Whereas Hindu and Buddhist texts portray mankind strapped to the wheel of rebirth by the thongs of karma, Dr Whitton's subjects present a more instructional view of karma's workings. Picture the entire human race at work in a cosmic classroom where, over the course of many lifetimes, we set ourselves lesson after lesson. Each one of us is both pupil and teacher and we have the power, through our actions, to direct our own course of learning. This is essentially the message of the *Brihadaranyaka Upanishad*:

> As a man acts, so does he become . . .
> As a man's desire is, so is his destiny.

Karmic patterns are formed as a result of the soul's efforts to improve itself with specific challenges. These patterns greatly influence personal choice and the planning of ensuing incarnations. In the between-life state the soul reviews its performance across many lifetimes and chooses to resolve or atone for certain deeds in the next life. While past mistakes confront the soul in the *bardo*, most karmic adjustments can only be made by returning to physical existence and re-encountering, in many instances, those with whom the karma has been established.

Historically, karma has undergone profound transformation in the past five thousand years. As handed down by the ancient Egyptians, karmic justice signified the ruthless balancing of a moral accounts book whereby bad deeds were met with matching retribution. 'Your deed turns into judgement of you,' declares verse twenty-eight of *The Instruction of Ptahhotep* which dates back to 2,000 BC. The Old and New Testaments were equally uncompromising and displayed an even keener taste for vengeance. Revelation 13:10 says: 'He that leadeth into captivity shall go into captivity; he that killeth with the sword must be killed with the sword.' The centuries that followed Jesus Christ saw a more sophisticated interpretation of the archaic law. The Christian Gnostics and the Hebrew Kabalists came to understand karma as a law of compensation. Anyone who killed another would not necessarily be condemned to die in similar circumstances but would be expected to make amends for the act in some way, perhaps by returning in a future life to care for the dying and the maimed.

A third interpretation, which extends to the present day and is thought to have originated in European mysticism during the middle ages, decrees that karma is simply a process of learning, a 'school of hard knocks' that instils knowledge through repetitive trial and error. To commit murder will set in motion events that may not necessitate either having to be a murderer's victim or having to make active compensation. Whatever the repercussions may be, they will teach the murderer that, by acting thus, he has only been self-destructive; by destroying another's physical body, he has merely retarded his own spiritual progress.

The past-life inventories of Dr Whitton's subjects tend to reflect all three interpretations of karma, 'an eye for an eye' being very much in evidence in the earlier stages of personal evolution. The subjects themselves, when carried to the between-life state, speak of karma as that which they have created for themselves as a means of progressively refining their natures. Time and time again they have asserted in trance that they must undergo certain experiences in order to purge imperfection and to further personal growth. How these experiences are handled determines how much progress is made and, if learning is not accomplished, the situation must be replayed. Practice makes perfect in the cosmic classroom. Let's look at some examples from Dr Whitton's casebook of how karmic necessity reaches across the centuries:

• Through past-life regression, Ben Garonzi re-experienced a succession of male and female lives in which he participated in vicious exchange by killing those who treated him badly. In this life, he has been plunged once more into a repugnant situation in which he has been tempted to opt for a violent solution. Severely brutalized as a child, Ben grew to hate his father so intensely that, at the age of eighteen, he came very close to killing him. One evening, when his father had become insensate from alcohol, Ben went to a kitchen drawer and pulled out a carving knife with every intention of slitting the man's throat. Then, listening to the promptings of an inner voice, he changed his mind and replaced the knife in the drawer. This decision to desist became a major turning point in Ben's life. From that moment on, he grew more outgoing, and he went on to pursue a career that brought administrative responsibilities.

In the interlife, Ben learned that he was embroiled in karmic circumstances that were designed to teach him to withstand extreme provocation without recourse to violence. He discovered that he had chosen his difficult childhood knowing he would be severely tested by a father who had figured prominently in a series of antagonistic relationships in previous incarnations. In the *bardo*, Ben was aware of a voice which said, 'If you do it right this time, things will work out all right. If not, you will require a learning environment of even greater intensity.'

Ben understood at once that by acting with restraint towards his father in the crucial incident with the carving knife, he had wrestled a karmic predicament into submission. By passing his own test, he had finally extricated himself from the pattern of error in life after life.

• A mother of three children whose husband was killed in an aeroplane crash in 1971 is paying directly for her actions of a thousand years ago. Under hypnosis, she saw herself as a religious leader in the Mayan civilization of Central America who delighted in sentencing to a sacrificial death anyone who disagreed with her. Today she is having to cope with the trials of bereavement she once foisted upon others. Metaconsciousness revealed that she had planned to develop compassion in this life.

• A Jewish surgeon, now retired, learned that he has been making compensation for past-life behaviour, specifically his cruelty towards the Jews when he was a Roman sergeant stationed in revolt-prone Judaea some time after the death of Christ. Dr Simon Ezra regained vivid memories of breaking the bodies of Jews half-buried in sand by charging over them on his horse. His karmic role in this life has been to mend bodies as well as to experience the rigours of persecution. Early in his career, soon after his first divorce, he was ostracized from practising in Toronto's major teaching hospitals because of his Jewish blood. Before he underwent hypnosis, Dr Ezra would occasionally terrorize the hospital nurses by thowing surgical instruments in petulant expression of his anger. His aggressive attitude softened considerably once he was able to appreciate the reasons for his choice of race and profession.

• An egocentric housewife discerned from the inter-life that her selfishness represented a karmic block that had proved troublesome for centuries. Hilary Jackson grasped that she had incarnated, in reverse order, as a narcissistic Southern belle in Georgia, an arrogant French priest and a Scotsman who, caring only for himself, ignored the needs of his family. Enlightened by what she saw, Hilary realized that to continue in this manner would be counter-productive. Accordingly she has revised her attitude of self-absorption and her once-doomed marriage has dramatically revived.

• Tony Kalamaris, a high school teacher who is striving to accommodate his interest in eroticism with deeply spiritual inclinations, learned in meta-consciousness of the karmic pattern that had precipi-tated his internal struggle. He was made aware that his ten most recent incarnations incorporated ex-tremes of sanctimonious and licentious behaviour and that his task was to integrate the spiritual and erotic aspects of his nature. He reports:

As I watched myself fluctuate from one extreme to another in different lives, I became quite annoyed with the process and exclaimed, 'I do not see the point of physical life!' Whereupon I was aware of an incredibly vivid woman's face, almost shocking in its clarity. This face told me that the erotic element provided the yeast for developing conscience, altruism and benevolent con-cern. Eroticism, being a rudimentary force that provokes interaction, forces people to become intimately involved and can therefore initiate and assist in spiritual development. This is what I had to learn because I had always seen sex and spirituality as separate from one another. This is what I must now put into practice.

• The momentum set up by past-life intimacy spanned more than 1,700 years in the case of Becky Roberts and her lover, Clive Edensor. In this life, Becky has struggled to raise three children with scarcely any help from her aloof and alcoholic husband. Yet the burden has been considerably lightened by a secret love relationship she enjoys with a man she first met some twenty years ago. Past-life investigation revealed that Clive Edensor, who has been unwaveringly loyal and supportive throughout Becky's domestic difficulties, is in the process of making karmic compensation.

When Becky was regressed to a lifetime in Alexandria in the third century AD she saw herself as a temple virgin in the Cult of Osiris. She also recognized Clive as a neophyte priest. Strongly attracted to one another, they fell in love and – although they were both sworn to celibacy – a passionate relationship ensued. One day their lovemaking was detected by the temple elders. The young priest claimed he had been seduced and the elders, accepting this story, allowed him to go free while condemning her to death. Because karma will not be denied, Clive is now making amends for his betrayal all those years ago.

As the last example illustrates, love and sex enliven the karmic process by stimulating human interaction. Many of Dr Whitton's subjects have traced their links with wives, husbands and lovers to a succession of previous lives and have perceived the karmic nature of these relationships.

The casework suggests that those who experienced a very positive relationship in a past life seek to renew that partnership. Whether the connection can be re-established in this life is often contingent upon whether a joint plan has been made in the between-life state. The case of Andrew Ormsby shows how failure to plan can lead to a life of emotional frustration. By the time Andrew met Maureen Richard, the entity who had been his lover in nineteenth-century England, Andrew was already married and his wife was expecting their first child. Nevertheless, this prior commitment could not prevent a loving relationship developing between himself and Maureen, a relationship which has continued, discreetly, for more than forty years.

In metaconsciousness, Andrew realized that he had failed to plan his current life because of his great reluctance to reincarnate. 'She [Maureen] is whispering in my ear,' he said in trance. 'But I don't want to come back.' Andrew was presented with an exceptionally vivid image of Maureen as she was in her last life, and he saw himself shrink from actively planning their reunion on the Earth plane. While karmic impetus has brought them together again, they have had to settle for a fugitive alliance rather than conjugal companionship.

Physical and psychological disorders and personal tragedies of all kinds can be attributed to karma. As the case study chapters will illustrate, moral deficiency and unresolved and repressed emotions are conferred on future incarnations in the form of disease, trauma, phobias and various other manifestations of difficulty. Hypnosis may shed light on specific karmic conditions and bring the realization – integral to the healing process – that the suffering has been self-willed. Karma's unfinished business will always pose problems and if there must be lamentation it can only be directed at ourselves. Writing in *Man and the World in the Light of Anthroposophy*, Stewart C. Easton declares . . .

> . . . Whenever we bemoan our destiny on Earth and complain of our ill-fortune, we are railing against *our own choice*, not the choice of some arbitrary god or gods who have done us a bad turn. In consequence, the one vice which no one with knowledge of karma should permit himself is *envy*, either envy of anyone else's life situation, or of his talents, fortune or friends. For we have what we have chosen and earned . . .

If we must endure a hard life, we are not *necessarily* coming to terms with misdemeanours from an earlier existence. By undergoing certain trials, we may be preparing ourselves for *future* tasks and accomplishments. Karma, despite its demands and implications, should not be considered as iron-clad destiny which forces us to act in a given manner. The very essence of karma implies the presence of motive which, in turn, necessitates the exercise of free will.

Karmic evolution embraces the development of personality and the refinement of skills and aptitudes. Dr Whitton has noticed how his subjects, in the course of many lifetimes, advance along a road that leads from the infantile and egocentric to the adolescent and, eventually, to the mature personality. Progress is always determined by strength of will. He has also seen how talents are worked on in incarnation after incarnation. An unusual facility in this life can be traced to a reincarnational history of effort and application. From this observation it is logical to assume that great statesmen, musicians, philosophers and others of world renown must have gradually learned and built upon their abilities in past lives until these abilities reach fruition in a life of influence. Alternatively a person with a dearth of leadership qualities and scant organizational flair is unlikely to have been a leader of historical significance in a previous life.

Karma is at work in every area of human endeavour. In his book *Wisdom of the Mystic Masters*, Joseph J. Weed observed the following expressions of cause and effect in the workings of karmic law:

- Aspirations and desires become abilities.

- Repeated thoughts become tendencies.

- Will to performance becomes action.

- Painful experiences become conscience.

- Repeated experiences lead to wisdom.

The trouble with karma is that it can obscure the soul's higher purpose even as its snakes and ladders provide the means for attainment of that purpose. The karmic cacophony that accompanies all personal striving and human interaction frequently drowns the background theme in our lives – the soul's inner struggle to know itself more clearly. To draw upon yet another metaphor, it is as though we are all driving automobiles along the grand highway of evolution only to have the destination obscured by the constant obstructions of karmic traffic jams. In the life between life, knowledge of higher purpose is always at hand. The earthly expression of the quest for the fulfilment of destiny, however, is awakened progressively in 'soul searching' that appears to advance through five distinct stages that may span many lifetimes. These stages are:

Materialism: The search for physical well-being, a state dominated by sensual craving. There is very little consideration for the feelings of others and philosophical goals are non-existent. There is no recognition of an afterlife or a supreme power of any kind.

Superstition: The first awareness that there are forces and entities greater than oneself. Practically nothing is known about this omniscient power; there is solely the appreciation that something is out there which cannot be controlled except, perhaps, by amulets and rituals. A materialistic lifestyle continues to prevail.

Fundamentalism: The practice of simple, superstitious and rigid thinking about God or the Almighty. Such thinking becomes the rationale for living. There is belief that prayer, adherence to ritual, and the practice of certain attitudes and behaviour will guarantee the supreme reward – a place in heaven or the afterlife. A leader is usually required to intercede with the all-powerful God, who must be appeased. It matters little whether the leader is a guru who wears a turban or is called Jesus Christ;

someone is needed to harness, direct, and expound upon basic conviction.

Philosophy: Early awakening to the awareness of self-responsibility. Religious conviction is maintained, but there is an appreciation that reliance on dogma will not suffice. This stage is marked by respect for life, tolerance of the beliefs of others, and an understanding of the deeper teachings of the orthodox religions.

Persecution: The prevalence of inner tension and anguish which springs from the intense desire to understand the hidden meaning of life. Awareness that there is a profound meaning and purpose to existence is fraught with uncertainty as to how such knowledge can be attained. The search for answers frequently takes the form of extensive reading, study, and membership of various mystical and metaphysical groups. The title of this stage is taken from Christ's Sermon on the Mount and the phrase 'Blessed are the persecuted' (Matthew 5:10).

When these neophyte stages have been successfully completed, the individual steps firmly on to a path of evolution. Evolution can be likened to a huge mountain criss-crossed with trails, some more travelled than others. These diverse paths may lead up the Eastern side through meditation and transcendent contemplation, or they may climb the Western face through mysticism and intellectual metaphysics.

So long as the desire remains to be, to do, or to possess, karmic consequence will continue. The better the law of momentum is understood, the more one can foresee precisely how personal motivations, attitudes and behaviour are constructing karmic conditions. Even Buddha, who derived much of his philosophy from the writings of Hindu sages, still suffered from the long arm of karma, much to the amazement of his disciples. On a day when a cactus thorn had entered his foot, strangers had spoken unkindly of him, and a quest for alms in a nearby village had left his begging bowl empty, Buddha was asked to explain his own karma as carried forward from other lives. He replied:

> . . . the bonds of karma, like true servants, ever attend on all creatures . . . Karma is like the stream of time. Never can its course be stopped in its constant pursuit of man. Long is the vine of karma; new, and yet always covered with old fruit; a wonderful companion of all creatures, and yet immovable, however you may pull it, grasp it, part it, uproot it, twist it, rub it, or skilfully break it into atoms, it is never destroyed.

Buddha was making it very clear that high attainment could neither evade nor nullify the mistakes of previous lives. A law is a law and there is no short cut to wisdom – the goal of karmic circumstance. '. . . Man's karma travels with him, like his shadow,' wrote Alan Watts in *The Spirit of Zen*. 'Indeed, it is his shadow, for it has been said, "Man stands in his own shadow and wonders why it is dark." ' For karma to end, old debts must be paid off and there must be no new indebtedness created. And the only way the account ledgers of many lifetimes may be balanced is through the wholehearted adoption of the precepts of love and selflessness. To quote once more from Joseph Weed:

As long as there is the slightest tinge of self in any of our actions, as long as we are good because we hope for reward, then we shall have to return here in order to receive that reward. Every cause has its effect, every action its fruit, and desire is the cord that links them. When this thread is broken and burned out, the connection will end and the soul will be free.

The most important conclusion to be drawn from the idea of karma is that chance has played no part in arranging the circumstances in which we find ourselves. On Earth, we are the personification of choices that have been made in the *bardo*. Our discarnate decision-making has assigned us to our situation in life and, through subconscious inclination, continues to bring forth the bouquets and brickbats of destiny. To be convinced of the truth of the law of karma is to endorse the state of affairs in which one has placed oneself, no matter how difficult it might be. The individual seeks out challenges and ordeals, knowing that they contain the greatest opportunities for learning and growth.

Karmic Case Studies

7

Power of the Will

'Seek and ye shall find;
knock, and it shall be
opened unto you.'

St Matthew (7:7)

Michael Gallander, PhD, was one of those rare individuals who had just about everything, or so it seemed to his fellow IBM researchers. Michael was brilliant, athletic, good-looking and likeable. Sharply analytical and fluent in his thinking, he was an electronics 'whiz' whose innovative mind had earned the respect of the top executives in the company. He was also a man who gave freely of his time and energy. Most days, Michael stuffed one pocket with coins for any drunks and down-and-outs who crossed his path; another pocket bulged with a plastic bag of yesterday's bread. This he fed to the pigeons nesting in the ravine a short walk away from his office.

Very few people knew – and none would have suspected – that Michael Gallander was inordinately troubled by inner conflicts beyond his understanding. Only Michael was aware how drastically the rewards of success and achievement had been undermined by sensations of guilt and self-loathing that clawed at his insides. Facing himself in the mirror each morning filled him with such revulsion that even as he shaved, the ugliness rose like bile. Perhaps this ugliness was connected with the suicidal tendencies that sometimes caused him to amble obliviously into the path of oncoming traffic. But Michael couldn't be sure. And he had no idea why he had been plagued for years by the most perplexing of symptoms ... he was overwhelmed by a sense of dread whenever he made love to his wife, Sharron.

Michael had struggled hard to succeed. Born of working-class, Jewish parents in the South Bronx, New York, he was disliked by his mother and largely ignored by a father who made his only son the target of screaming rages. This childhood of emotional tyranny and verbal abuse left Michael thoroughly inhibited by his late teens. He felt threatened by the outside world and often shied away from contact with strangers. So pronounced was his self-consciousness that, on several occasions when his car needed fuel, he shrank from driving into a petrol station for fear of having to talk with the attendant.

Although he managed to do very well at school and university, Michael found that, by his early twenties, he was fast becoming inundated by a mounting inventory of phobias, anxieties and inhibitions. From the start, he was determined to battle his difficulties no matter how trying they became. And it was this resolve that led him to embark on a programme of orthodox psychotherapy that was to last fifteen years. As his career led him from city to city, three analysts – in St Louis, Missouri, Cleveland, Ohio and New York – gradually managed to relieve Michael of certain basic fears and insecurities related to his disturbed upbringing. But none was able to explain, let alone banish, his ubiquitous feelings of guilt and self-hatred and the dread he always experienced with Sharron. Never before, during teenage sexual encounters with other partners who preceded his courtship with Sharron, had he faced this problem. It was only when he approached his wife that he felt himself in the grip of a seemingly irrational fear that she would suffer because of his lovemaking.

Michael had other afflictions, too. The trio of analysts was unable to establish why he nursed a chronic fear of being buried alive, a fear welling up into random panic attacks that brought heavy perspiration and hyper-ventilation. Or why, even though loud noises couldn't wake him, he would throw off the bed covers and sit bolt upright in alarm at the faintest whisper or the most gentle tip-toeing. Or why he was terrified of losing his temper. Or why, since early childhood, he had been troubled by a recurring fantasy involving the murder of a woman in a white gown. Or why a rash flared intermittently on the backs of his upper arms. The raw itchiness would erupt without warning; it could strike in any situation at any time and usually lasted for a matter of minutes. As a young boy, he had walked into his parents' bedroom to encounter his mother musing, naked, before a mirror. Disconcerted, she had grabbed him by the backs of the arms, shaking him and shrieking admonitions. Each of the analysts seized upon this disclosure, claiming to have uncovered the source of the problem ... but the rash wouldn't go away.

During one visit to his psychiatrist in St Louis, Michael remembers contemplating the rash as he waited for the therapeutic session to begin. For a moment, he had an image of himself – not as Michael Gallander but as a separate being that appeared to share his identity. This separate self was pushing someone who was clutching his arms precisely where the inflammation appeared. When the consultation began, however, he made no mention of this disquieting image. He thought his analyst would say he was crazy.

When Michael was transferred to Toronto he was thirty-eight years old and understandably weary of subjecting himself to analysis that, while helpful for the first few years, was clearly unequal to the challenge of the abiding poison within. Still obsessed with the need to plumb his conflicts to their very depths, he doggedly believed that relief from his prolonged emotional suffering was available some-how, somewhere. Consequently, he cast about for an alternative – a new, deeper way of being, of perceiv-ing. He delved into astrology and mysticism and the ancient wisdom of the East. In time, his search led him to a meeting of the Toronto Society for Psychical Research, where Dr Joel Whitton happened to be delivering a lecture on the metaphysical implications of reincarnation. Invigorated by what he heard, Michael approached Dr Whitton, told how his rash had resisted fifteen years of therapeutic minis-trations and asked whether it could possibly be explained in terms of past-life experience. This time, he *knew* he wasn't going to be called crazy.

So it was that, on a bitterly cold day in February 1979, Michael found himself waiting apprehensively for his first session with Dr Whitton. Michael wasn't sure whether he believed in reincarnation. Until attending the lecture, he hadn't really given the idea much thought. All he knew was that Dr Whitton occasionally dealt with his patients' difficulties by hypnotically regressing them to 'past lives'. And Michael was willing to try anything.

The first session yielded little. With his lanky frame sprawled across Dr Whitton's red leather couch, Michael succumbed, after repeated prompting, to a deep trance. When asked about an immediate past life, he murmured a reply, settling tentatively on the year 1915 ... then drew away hastily as if he had touched a red hot iron in his mind. Trembling, Michael broke trance without even realizing what he had seen. And although he was coaxed once more into the hypnotic state, nothing could persuade him to pursue his connection with that year; Dr Whitton's gentle probing was sternly resisted by his subject's subconscious mind. The emotional and therapeutic significance of this initial flashpoint was to elude both doctor and patient for years.

Michael's resistance retreated steadily in the sessions that followed, allowing him glimpses of former existences. Preferring to lie on Dr Whitton's broadloom rug rather than the couch, he revised his self-perception by inspecting a parade of personalities from the past. He saw himself as Gustavus, a Swedish itinerant carpenter at work in the churches of

Cologne at the time of the Reformation. As Henri, a sixteenth-century French cotton merchant anxious about Turkish raids on his ships, he experienced – or re-experienced – symptoms of that middle-aged man's angina: chest pains and shortness of breath. He also spoke with a distinctive accent and uttered several words of archaic French. In gradually acclimatizing to the trance state, Michael instinctively accepted these characters as himself, a self that had evidently materialized in different incarnations. But it wasn't until he found himself back, way back, in the year 1216 that he was affected by more than mere fascination. Suddenly, his awareness was jarred with the most visceral of sensations . . .

> On the brow of a hill stands a castle, its massive stone walls enclosing a tangibly repulsive atmosphere. Restlessly moving about a gloomy anteroom is the source of these negative emanations – a powerful, imposing man of harsh aspect and miserable disposition. He is a knight in late middle age, a Teutonic knight called Hildebrandt von Wesel, the lonely ruler of a small principality in southeast Westphalia. His life has been irredeemably barbarous and, because idealistic impulses grant him no reprieve, he is consumed with guilt, self-hatred and paranoia. But still he clings to his illusions. 'I am the Arm of God!' he yells at Dr Whitton in a rasping voice. 'I am the Arm of God!'

Within Hildebrandt, it seemed, lay a wealth of important material and, in subsequent sessions, Dr Whitton regressed Michael to various stages of the knight's existence. What Michael saw wasn't pleasant – in fact it was downright horrifying – but, sometimes, he experienced almost pleasurable after-effects. A tentative feeling of internal consolidation told him that a tangled skein of repression, *his* repression, was being unravelled. It was an unravelling that fifteen years of painstaking analysis had failed to precipitate. But then, why would Michael, or the specialists he engaged, have suspected that many of his problems remained because their genesis took place not in infancy, but in former incarnations?

Like a man cleaning a huge pane of glass with a toothpick rolled in cotton wool, Dr Whitton rubbed away at the screen of Michael's buried memories, trying to make them gleam again. He was endeavouring not only to retrieve but also to analyse the Michael Gallander of eight hundred years ago. While it took a long time to glean a composite account of Hildebrandt's life, Dr Whitton was aware from the very beginning that he was dealing with a man capable of great evil . . .

Hildebrandt has left his principality far behind. In 1189, at thirty-one years of age, he is a knight commander with the Third Crusade stationed with his soldiers in the desert near Acre, Palestine. The proud Teuton, wearing white robes emblazoned with a black cross, curses the intolerable heat as a group of Arab women are prodded before him, pleading for their lives. But their entreaties have no effect on Hildebrandt who glares disdainfully at the captives. All around, the desert is littered with suits of armour belonging to fellow knights, slaughtered in battle. These brave, loyal men had been like brothers to him and his inclination is to weep openly at their loss. Instead, fearing to betray these feelings, Hildebrandt resorts to barbarism. He orders his men to place the diminutive women inside the suits of armour where, pinned to the sand like giant

steel crabs, they are baked alive in the hot sun. Their
screams are powerless to save them.

Michael was shaking and perspiring when he regained normal consciousness, but the upheaval produced results within hours. For the first time since
childhood he found he was no longer burdened with
a fear of being buried alive.

Over the next few months, Michael was to observe
the vile litany of Hildebrandt's crimes. Once he actually felt himself in the knight's body, on horseback,
watching a woman with a baby in her arms begging
to be spared. 'I am staring at her the way someone
else might stare at a worm,' he later recounted. 'No
sympathy, no compassion.' The act of lowering his
lance and running it through the infant and into the
mother brought him out of trance with tears running
down his cheeks. He knew that he was responsible
but wanted neither to accept nor to believe what he
had seen. He also knew that as Michael Gallander
he was incapable of such callousness. Leaving Dr
Whitton's office that day, he wandered distractedly
into a nearby park where he stopped to feed the
pigeons. Watching the birds swoop and strut to claim
the scattered pieces of bread, he wondered how this
same man of gentle instincts could have killed a
helpless woman. Then again, he reminded himself,
even Adolf Hitler loved dogs.

Michael's first year of sessions with Dr Whitton
was not yet over when, after much resistance, he
encountered Hildebrandt as a twelve-year-old. This
time, however, his attention moved pointedly to
other players in the grim medieval drama. Hildebrandt's parents were more than familiar . . . they

were his parents in the current lifetime. Circumstances hadn't been so very different for him in twelfth-century Westphalia – here he was, born of a loveless union which had pitched him into a disturbed childhood. His feelings of rejection sometimes tipped over into active antagonism . . .

Hildebrandt's father is teaching his son how to wield a sword. The boy, brimming with past resentment, senses his opportunity and stabs his father in the eye. Some weeks later, the grievously injured ruler dies of a brain abscess. Everyone believes his death is accidental, but Hildebrandt knows better . . .

With every session, Michael learned more . . .

Hildebrandt's mother is a manipulative woman who schemes and conspires to ensure her interests are successfully navigated through the cross-currents of court intrigue. At age thirteen, Hildebrandt is considered to be on the threshold of manhood and only a short period of time separates him from control of the principality which measures, in breadth, 'a day's ride through the forest'. His incipient maturity, however, makes him sexually attractive to his mother who, not content with a string of affairs in the court, makes playful advances towards her son. This inveigling so repulses the young prince that he reacts by pushing his mother ever closer to the edge of a tall flight of stone steps. In the ensuing struggle, the failed seductress plunges down the steps, breaking her neck. As she falls to her death, she grasps vainly at her son's arms, leaving his triceps badly scratched . . .

Once this episode had been recalled, Michael's troublesome rash would never recur. Something was happening; some kind of slow thaw seemed to be at work in the icebox of his psyche. It was all very encouraging, but there was so much more to experience as Hildebrandt and others. Another nine months of sessions were required to elicit a step-by-step account of the knight's disastrous love match . . .

Just before Hildebrandt inherits his kingdom, he meets and falls in love with a girl named Rachael, the daughter of a literate Jew (none of Hildebrandt's family can read or write) who serves as court physician. At about the same time, the prince is being heavily influenced by a court monk who, having manœuvred Hildebrandt's parents for years, has little difficulty in manipulating the son and heir. While Hildebrandt and Rachael think they have managed to keep their relationship secret, the monk's spies discover not only that the pair are passionate partners but also that Rachael is pregnant. Consequently, the monk suspects that Rachael will ask Hildebrandt to marry her and, abhorring such a union as sacrilegious, he plants a seed of distrust in Hildebrandt's mind. He insinuates that Rachael wants matrimony so that she can steal the throne. 'And you cannot marry a Jew,' the monk tells the ruler-to-be. 'They are the accursed of God; you must arrange a proper political marriage.'

Now Hildebrandt is an idealistic youth keenly aware of his inability to convert his idealism into action. Wanting to impress his will upon the world, he nevertheless feels like a reed shaken by the wind of circumstance. And so when Rachael breaks the news that she is carrying his child, the prince explodes with the realization that yet again events are dictating the course of his life. Anticipating the very scheme proposed by the monk, he flies into a rage.

Hildebrandt's fury and frustration are so great that he hits Rachael hard in the stomach and crushes her neck with his large hands. Then, in one swift movement, he dashes her against the buttress of a castle balcony, tipping her over the battlements and into the moat below. In the state of shock that follows, Hildebrandt looks down disbelievingly on the body of his loved one, half-submerged in the stinking, refuse-strewn water. Gasping, choking and vomiting, he staggers back from the battlements to block from his mind all that has happened. Indeed, so strenuous is this act of repression that his knuckles are clenched until they start to bleed.

When he emerges at last from this numbing withdrawal, Hildebrandt is unnervingly quiet and self-contained. It is as if Rachael has never existed . . .

This repression breeds a neurosis that transforms him into an obsessive Christian zealot who, as local organizer for the Third Crusade, twists his self-loathing into vengeance against the Moslems in the Holy Land. He would grant no mercy because he could feel none . . .

There were moments during the dramatic re-enactment of Rachael's murder when Dr Whitton, despite his experience in handling emotional intensity during trance sessions, was concerned lest Michael's contortions provoke a heart attack. Nevertheless both doctor and patient weathered the storms of Hildebrandt's trauma and Michael found himself panting on the broadloom as normal consciousness returned, wondering how much more he could bear to witness. Drained and devastated by these gut-wrenching episodes from his deep past, he at least understood why, in this life, he felt a compulsive need to punish himself. Not only had he been responsible for the most wretched violence, he had killed none other than Sharron, his wife. For there was no doubt in his mind that Sharron and Rachael were elements of the same soul joined to his own deeds and misdeeds by the unspeakably long arm of karma. This connection was corroborated when Sharron subsequently entered trance and was carried back into a life as Rachael. She recovered vivid memories of her murder by Hildebrandt . . .

It was a warm spring evening. I was in a bedroom with an opening leading out to a parapet. I was arguing with Hildebrandt and moving from the parapet to the bedroom and back again to the parapet. We were both dressed in loose gowns. Hildebrandt wore tights or hose and a shirt under his gown. I was wearing nothing under mine.

We were hitting at each other and screaming. This yelling was in a language that I didn't understand and, when I tried to catch the meaning it was as if English had been dubbed over some of the words. Hildebrandt shouted at me, 'You whore Jewess! No Jew bastard will inherit from me!'

We were finally both out on the parapet and Hilde-brandt punched me hard in the stomach. I doubled over and blood dribbled from the side of my mouth. Then he grabbed me around the throat and started to strangle me. He continued strangling and I went limp. He thrust me across the balustrade and something snapped in my back. He released me with a slight shove and my body fell over the balustrade and into the moat where I lay face up, my hair loose and floating, tangled with scum and debris.

Later, in the courtyard of the castle, a group of women carried my body on some sort of bier. My face was exposed, but the rest of my body, even my hair, was completely swathed in white material.

Now that Michael had seen the terrifying results of Hildebrandt's failure to control his temper, his fears about becoming uncontrollably angry gradually abated. So did his tendency to be startled awake by the slightest sounds. Michael had observed that loud noises from the courtyard didn't disturb the sleeping Hildebrandt who, perpetually wary of assassination, was always roused abruptly by the most surreptitious of sounds. Michael was Hildebrandt – and yet he didn't have to be. He didn't have to hold on to the knight's patterns of behaviour. Dr Whitton, meanwhile, had every intention of continuing to tug at the curtain drawn across Michael's repertoire of previous existences. First he decided on another approach . . .

'Go back,' he urged his hypnotized subject. 'Go back to the time just before you were born as the knight.'

Michael was speechless for a long time. From the sporadic twitching of his facial muscles and the flickering of his eyelids, he seemed to be in thrall to vistas of this other world, the mysterious void between incarnations. When at last he spoke, his words recalled the old adage about the road to hell being paved with good intentions. For his life as Hildebrandt had been planned as an infinitely more positive and enlightening experience than the heinous incarnation that followed. Michael's voice rang with ardent optimism . . .

'I am one with the universe. I am one with the stars and am very excited about being born. I will attempt to build . . . a land without a boundary. I will be a fine king with wise advisers and I will encourage barter and study and travel.'

As he heard himself make this pronouncement, Michael realized, with some relief, that Hildebrandt was no Adolf Hitler after all. Through sheer impulsiveness, the knight had surrendered his lofty aspirations. Possessing high ideals, yet being pathetically incapable of living up to them, Hildebrandt degenerated into a driven and tortured human being rather than an essentially evil one. Now Michael was instructed to vault forward to the interlife that succeeded the death of Hildebrandt . . .

'What do you see?' inquired Dr Whitton.

Silent at first, Michael soon began to sob uncontrollably. He mumbled about his wrongdoing as Hildebrandt, touching on the time he impaled the mother and child on his lance. This only provoked more sobbing of heartbreaking intensity. His self-reproach was beyond the reach of reassurance.

'What do you see?' Dr Whitton asked once more. Slowly, painfully, Michael replied . . .

> 'It is black and I will not look. There was much I could have done, but I did not. I could have done so much good, but . . . I did not.'

To experience remorse in the life between lives is to experience a form of hell. For there is a time – quite early on, according to most subjects – when guilt comes home to roost in all its raw ugliness, stripped of the rationalizations and excuses we all employ to explain away our failings. This hell, however, is not eternal damnation. When the past life is assessed, the compassionate encouragement of the judgement board allows us to perceive even our most reprehensible actions with a degree of sympathy.

No matter how misused the immediate past life has been, the oversoul knows there's always another chance to make amends. And so Michael, while semi-slumbering in the *bardo*, acknowledged the neurotic flaw in his development and planned for himself an incarnation as Magnus – a priest living in 'Poland near Muscovy' during the first half of the fifteenth century. This new life was designed to afford a special opportunity to achieve greater self-control. Later Michael examined Magnus' life under hypnosis and saw that, in accordance with Church requirements, the priest had succeeded in stemming his innate aggression and suppressing his sexuality.

There were times when Michael felt at the mercy of his reincarnational experiences. Nightmares intruded on his sleep, and his days were spent turning over the revelations and conjectures that bubbled up in the wake of the hypnotic sessions. But by May 1981 the nightmares and the insights they produced had ceased. So had the past lives. No matter how hard they tried, doctor and patient found themselves blocked from further exploration. Because Michael was parrying every inquiring thrust, Dr Whitton knew there was, at the very least, one more hidden life which held secrets crucial to the remedial process. Eventually the existence of another critical incarnation was intimated, but all Michael would divulge was a first name – Victor – which meant absolutely nothing on its own. This hiatus had lasted for several fruitless months when Michael received an invitation to visit Maisie Newman's home in Cape Anne, Massachusetts. Maisie, a professional colleague, had offered her property several times to Michael and Sharron as a vacation base for touring the New England coast. They had never acted on the offer, but this time she was particularly insistent and Michael was frustrated enough with his past-life investigations to want to get away.

Ensconced in the seaside home after flying to Boston, the Gallanders rented a car and decided to drive the short distance to the old town of Salem. For a while they walked about the harbour town infamous for its seventeenth-century witchcraft trials. Then they felt drawn to enter a small reference library where Michael idly picked up an old book on the history of witchcraft in the area. All at once, he was struck by an intensely disquieting sensation that soon became strangely physical. 'It was as if something was shaking me,' he later recalled. 'I stood there trembling and perspiring. Something was at work in the back of my mind ... something I couldn't understand.' Michael was unaware of having any personal connection either with the book or with any of the material it contained; he knew only that his apparently boundless capacity for self-loathing had been aggravated. And that, surely, was significant. Leaving Salem and shaking off the brooding malignance, Michael couldn't wait to get back to Toronto for the next hypnotic session in which he was to confront the reappearance of guilt, sex and religion . . .

Victor Bracknell lives on a farm in New England. He is a staunchly puritanical moralist who believes that pleasure actively hinders the spiritual progress of those aspiring to enter the Kingdom of Heaven. It so happens that Victor's wedding day is fast approaching and, with it, the dilemma of how carnal ecstasy must be subdued.

Being a locksmith by trade, he fashions a tube-like metal device with a hole punctured at one end, a device he believes will allow him to inseminate his wife while reducing their mutual enjoyment to the absolute minimum. On their wedding night, this instrument severely injures the bride's vaginal area. Victor quickly panics and tries unsuccessfully to staunch the bleeding. Within a few hours, his wife is dead ...

Breaking the trance, Michael shook convulsively on Dr Whitton's floor as he grappled, at uncomfortably close quarters, with the deathly potential of the act of love. He couldn't help but compare Victor with Hildebrandt. Both had rashly and misguidedly killed their loved ones, though Hildebrandt seemed by far the more malevolent of the two. In a subsequent session, however, Michael learned that Victor embodied his sexual neurosis at its most perverse ...

After burying his wife in the woods and telling all who inquire as to her whereabouts that she simply ran away on their wedding night, Victor shuns all memory of the fatal incident. Later Victor's sexual disturbance, driven by strong guilt feelings, draws him to Salem in 1692 where he takes vicarious pleasure in watching women convicted of witchcraft die on the gallows. Not content with being an ardent spectator, he ensures that one pathetic old woman is sentenced to death by bearing false witness against her.

Michael – who in this life is incapable of telling a serious untruth – shuddered at remembrance of his recent visit to Salem and, as he did so, began to wonder whether the horror would ever cease. He was now only too conversant with karma's endurance and interplay as he scanned the threads of hundreds of years of his past lives stretched across the loom of eternity. It was almost as if he could see them being woven into a cohesive, if disturbing, cord. And although this helped him to understand better the anguish of his current life, it was hardly comforting to know that each successive existence added to, rather than lightened, the karmic burden. 'The Eternal runs one hell of a high school,' he gasped between trances during one particularly rigorous session.

Further dredging of Michael's subconsciousness scooped up more ugliness. He was Angela Fiore, a peasant girl from a tiny village near Genoa who became the brutalized mistress of an officer in Napoleon's occupying army in 1809. He was also Robert Macready, a scholarly English gentleman of late Victorian times who, fraught with guilt and sexual neuroses, indulged so excessively in alcohol and drugs that he died, pallid and frail, after walking in front of a carriage in his early forties. In Robert's slide into delirium, Michael was quick to perceive echoes of the unconscious suicidal tendencies that haunted his own life. He was prone to 'become absent-minded', as he put it, and had been 'awakened' several times in the middle of the street by blaring car horns or an alarmed pedestrian's tug on his arm.

Yet there were encouraging signs that Michael was undergoing deep and positive change. Although the guilt and sense of dread maintained their obstinacy, he was more intuitive, more assertive and more at ease, both with himself and with others. Perhaps most encouraging of all, Dr Whitton was displaying all the contained excitement of a tracker dog hot on the scent. After more than three years of probing

Michael's reincarnational history, he sensed he was ready to sneak up on a life that should, with luck, be the catalyst that would release eight centuries of bottled-up emotion. He remembered how Michael had, in the very first session, touched upon and then recoiled from the year 1915 and, in hope of circumventing this resistance, he decided to steer him into the interlife prior to this immediate past life. In what Dr Whitton now regards as the case's most crucial session, he coaxed his subject into meta-consciousness and waited patiently as his face became suffused with the wonder and the bewilderment common to all who trespass in the *bardo*. Dr Whitton allowed several minutes to pass before he asked the first question:

'What will you be born as?' . . . There was a long pause.

  '*A woman.*'

'And what will be the purpose of your next life?' . . . Another long pause.

  '*To make preparation for the next entity in the soul's learning process. To repay karma.*'

Further questioning revealed that Michael's soul was counselled in the interlife to attempt – no matter how great the earthly penalty – to resolve the conflicts that had wreaked so much havoc over so many lifetimes. The agenda indicated the orchestration of sexual trauma as well as an intent to break away from dogmatic religious attitudes. If all went according to plan, this next life would be a tough yet pivotal incarnation, a life that would sharply reverse the steady accumulation of indebtedness.

For Michael Gallander, veteran of the trance state that he was, the next few sessions would prove to be the most arduous of them all. Reassured by his visit to the interlife, he began to tackle – often hesitatingly and never willingly – traumatic episodes from the life of Julia Murchison, who was born in 1910 into a God-fearing, poverty-stricken family in rural Kentucky. Time and time again, Michael's body arched and thrashed across Dr Whitton's floor as he confronted what he hadn't wanted to remember. Screaming, weeping, protesting and sighing in voices that ranged in timbre from those of a small child to a young woman, he chronicled the events of Julia's brief but highly purposeful existence . . .

After the premature death of her mother, Julia is raised by her father, a drunkard who habitually beats and torments her. Brutally raped by this man at the age of five, she represses the event – 1915 was, after all, the year from which Michael had fled – and grows up deeply troubled. Nevertheless she's a wilful, plucky girl who makes a conscious decision to pull away from the constrictions of her Southern Baptist community. Leaving home at the earliest opportunity, she heads for Louisville where, while dreaming of travelling to California to star in the silent movies, she works as a waitress and then as a prostitute. Her childhood rape had left her unable to achieve orgasm, and it is her unconscious determination to recover the memory of this traumatic incident that leads her into prostitution. But working as a whore fails to produce the primal experience she needs. So, despite her loathing for her father, she lays plans to seduce him hoping – again unconsciously –

that a repetition of her childhood rape will cause her to rediscover the past and learn from its lessons. 'Maybe I'll be able to feel,' Dr Whitton is told in a wistful Southern accent.

Julia, now in her twenties, is wearing a provocative white petticoat in readiness for her father when he next visits Louisville for a church service. It's early on a Sunday afternoon when she hears him stumble on the outside steps leading up to her second-floor flat and, sure enough, he's drunk when he opens the door to her shouted 'Come in!' Standing unsteadily in her hallway, he senses the intended seduction and has a feeling that it's nothing but a tease. As he starts to get angry Julia keeps pouting and giggling, pouting and giggling. He tells her to stop, but she does nothing of the kind. Provoked beyond the desire for sex, he pulls a knife, rushes at her, and stabs her to death . . .

In the healing of any traumatic neurosis, there's an element that demands repetition of the causative event to bring the trauma into the conscious mind. Demonstrating its occurrence within a lifetime, Sigmund Freud labelled this phenomenon 'the compulsion to repeat'. Dr Whitton's case studies show, further, that the principle holds good from lifetime to lifetime. Making conscious, under hypnosis, a traumatic event which took place in a previous existence can lead to cessation of physical and psychological disorders. Blindly Julia sought this repetition in working as a prostitute and, when it couldn't be found, she obeyed the compulsion initiated by her interlife experience to search for a more drastic repeat performance. Julia miscalculated – not expecting to be killed as she was about to act out her childhood rape. In this life, Michael has retrieved those painful memories which explained, at last, his fantasy about the murder of a woman in a white gown.

Being Julia was unpleasant in the extreme but, as the sessions edged towards completion, Michael felt the oppression of centuries drain from his body, leaving him with a hitherto unknown sensation of well-being. No longer was his relationship with Sharron fraught with a sense of dread; his guilt and self-loathing ebbed away, and all absent-minded inclination to do away with himself evaporated. He discovered he could look into the mirror each morning without despairing and, when he fed the pigeons and gave money to derelicts on the street, he found he was motivated by joy as well as by compassion. Friends and relatives detected changes in Michael's attitude towards life. He managed to shed a puritanical predisposition towards leisure and pleasure that enabled him to relax more easily and feel freer within himself when, for example, he danced with his wife. Sharron, who accepts her role in Michael's reincarnational history, could hardly believe her husband's transformation. 'He's been freed from preoccupation,' she said. 'His mind is no longer his jailer.'

There were other dividends. In becoming aware of his personal tapestry of cause and effect spanning eight hundred years, Michael discovered that his concept of reality had been thoroughly overhauled. 'I have been allowed,' he said, speaking of his visits to the interlife, 'the barest glimpse of levels of creation that are far above anything I can even begin to put into words. I was made to feel that everything that we do has meaning at the highest level. Our sufferings are not random; they are merely part of an eternal plan more complex and awe-inspiring than we are capable of imagining.'

Final visits to the interlife – this time the period straddling the incarnations as Julia and Michael – further illuminated the nature of Michael's recovery. Before he was born, Michael was advised that his life's purpose would best be served by choosing the same parents he had had as Hildebrandt and by renewing the important relationship with Rachael. The resulting interaction with these individuals could help bring about the necessary awareness of his intended path. Furthermore he was counselled that he must persevere until he finally understood, and solved, his difficulties. Notwithstanding this advice, Michael's oversoul, presumably discouraged by past failures, planned the current incarnation without anticipating the rapid progress that was to follow.

Comparing his life's performance so far with his interlife observations, Michael realized that sketchy plans made for future incarnations had been brought forward to the present life to keep pace with the accelerated speed with which he was dispatching the challenges of his karmic script. In other words, Michael had managed to live several lifetimes within one incarnation, an achievement open to all who pursue their destiny with exceptional vigour. Within one incarnation, he has achieved results that, ordinarily, would require the labour of lifetimes.

Michael's desire to get well – so vital to the eventual success of the therapeutic process – sprang directly from Julia's determined, though doomed, efforts at self-therapy. As Manly P. Hall writes in *Death to Rebirth*, 'The individual pays his karma very largely by the process which perpetuates an attitude existing at a particular time. If this attitude exists at the time of the previous death, it will go on to become the drive for the re-embodiment of the new personality.'

Michael Gallander's karmic case study shows that what remains undone in one life can always be completed in the next incarnation, assuming, of course, that there's an abundance of willpower. By harnessing his power of will to seek out, acknowledge and transcend his crimes and conflicts, Michael has freed himself to pursue the idealism expressed in the interlife before he was reborn as Hildebrandt.

8

Allergic to Life?

'Extreme remedies are very
appropriate for extreme diseases.'

Hippocrates,
Aphorisms

'My body is a wreck and my life is in tatters,' Heather
Whiteholme told Dr Whitton when they first met in
the spring of 1979. This lament was supported by
a medical record which chronicled the failure of
conventional medicine to halt her steady, if mysterious, slide into physical disintegration.

Heather looked deceptively healthy. Her cheery
disposition and rosy complexion belied the fact that
her body was a battleground of allergic reactions
which impaired her hearing with constant ringing in
the ears and delivered pounding headaches, chest and
throat congestion, massive rashes and skin blisters.
The simple act of breathing put her at risk, discomfort usually succeeding exposure to such workaday influences as dust, pollen, cat fur, cigarette

smoke, dairy products, angora sweaters, perfume, paints and detergents. 'I cannot help but feel,' forty-four-year-old Heather admitted shyly, 'that I'm allergic to life itself.'

These troubles were compounded by repeated attacks of pneumonia and bronchitis, which left her bedridden for most of the winter, spring and fall. Ever since Heather and her biologist husband, Philip, had moved to Toronto from Mexico City in 1977, the attacks had worsened in response to the Canadian winters. Yet the Whiteholmes had only left the murky Mexican capital because a specialist had warned Heather: 'Get out of here – or the smog will kill you within five years.' The specialist was just one of a long retinue of doctors and medical consultants who had been presented with Heather's predicament. One medic pronounced her body to be in a 'state of war' while conceding the role of peacemaker was beyond him; another ordered complete rest for six months so that Heather's system might have a chance to recuperate from its 'total exhaustion'. There was a seemingly endless succession of X-rays and blood and urine tests which determined nothing and led nowhere. Meanwhile the sickly decline continued as doctor after doctor prescribed vast quantities of medication – allergy pills, antibiotics, antihistamines and cortisones – which were often of negligible benefit and, in some cases, provoked fresh allergic reactions.

Heather also suffered from severe psychological problems. Lacking self-esteem, she was easily intimidated and extremely susceptible to criticism. This overwhelming sense of inadequacy had caused her to abandon a promising career as a jewellery designer.

Every time she made the effort to create, she felt compelled to withdraw from her workspace because she dreaded the prospect of failure. Her fearfulness was only heightened by periodic black depressions that advanced 'like waves of rolling water'. These depressions – which always struck when she was happiest – had flooded her sensibilities since her university years. Incidentally, Heather wasn't about to take anti-depressants to help lift her mood – she was allergic to them!

Taking stock of Heather's acute vulnerability, Dr Whitton knew that the trend towards total incapacitation must be quickly reversed. Aiming to locate and eradicate the linchpin of her sickness, he first ordered a series of medical tests which revealed that Heather was indeed suffering from severe, intractable allergies exacerbated by an unusually low resistance to bronchitis and pneumonia. Taking into account Heather's emotional problems, Dr Whitton formed the tentative opinion that – for the sake of her sanity – she must have repressed her psychological difficulties only for them to reappear in the form of physical disorders.

Before hypnotic regression is even contemplated, Dr Whitton usually engages his patients in protracted consultations so that every relevant detail may be gleaned about the life at hand. But the urgency of Heather's case dictated otherwise. Together, doctor and patient opted for a headlong dive into Heather's past lives in the hope of awakening a trauma that held great therapeutic significance for the current existence.

Heather showed herself to be a remarkably good trance subject. So good, in fact, that as she lay in bed on the night after her first session, she copied Dr Whitton's technique and managed to hypnotize herself, much to her own initial terror. It wasn't long, however, before self-hypnosis became a familiar routine. To save consultation time and improve her chances of recovery, it was decided that Heather should explore her unconscious memories in trance at home and submit her findings in diary form for discussion at weekly sessions with Dr Whitton.

Heather's first few attempts to peer inside her unconscious mind were far from rewarding. But persevering until her inner eye was trained to pierce all obscurity, she was rewarded with a superabundance of material – all in glorious 3-D visions – that reached back through recorded history into the caveman era. Making sense of the imagery was another matter altogether. 'You're like a big Mack truck that dumps its load in my lap,' Dr Whitton told her as he glanced over sheaves of diary transcripts weaving tales of seemingly irrelevant past-life action mixed with fantasy and untold imaginings. This 'dumping' went on for nearly six weeks and Dr Whitton was pondering a change of direction when, early one morning, Heather settled into her favourite armchair, counted herself down into self-hypnotic trance, and found . . . Isobel.

There was something very sad and wistful about Isobel Drummond. Tall and slender, her long, dark hair swept into a chignon at the nape of her neck, she wore a full-length dress of pink chiffon with double-ruffled sleeves. Moving gracefully through the living room of a beautifully-furnished English home, she seated herself before a black grand piano and began to play, exquisitely, Chopin's piano Études . . .

Heather, who could hear Isobel's recital as clearly as if the piano were in the same room, was crying bitterly when she emerged from self-hypnosis. Never before had she felt such pressing identification with any other individual encountered while in trance. She *knew* Isobel had borne her soul identity in a different body not so very many years ago. But she didn't know why the sight and sound of this young woman should make her so thoroughly unhappy. Dr Whitton seized on this dilemma when Heather next visited his office. 'Why does Isobel make you so depressed?' he inquired. 'Find her again . . . and follow her until you can answer this question.'

Heather thought of little else but Isobel for the rest of the day. She was still wondering why Isobel depressed her when, late that night, she went to turn off the bedroom light before clambering into bed. Her hand was resting gently on the light switch when a sudden, shuddering impact made her gasp . . . her entire body was slammed internally by the most brutal shock. 'I cannot describe the feeling,' Heather said later, 'except to say that it was just like being in a very nasty motor accident in one's own home.' Initially she had no idea of the nature of the collision. Then she was very much aware of being in Isobel's body. She was lying on the ground, her right side was on fire, and she knew, in her terror, that the car in which she was travelling had careered over a cliff. The year was 1931 . . .

This emotional thunderbolt, which lasted only for a second or two, left Heather in a state of breakdown well beyond the reach of her husband's words of comfort and reassurance. All through the night, she wept intermittently as her conscious mind refused to relinquish the horrific scene. At five o'clock that morning, with husband Philip having finally succumbed to slumber, she wandered into the study, sat down before her typewriter, and tapped out these words: 'Have been shaking. Totally unable to sleep.' Her ordeal didn't end there. For the next three days, a combination of sleeplessness, nausea, sobbing, raw nerves and a harsh bronchial cough left Heather miserable and withdrawn. A diary entry made at 4.20 A.M. on Saturday, September 1, 1979, announced:

I have had to cancel all my daily plans. How do I tell my friends that I am suffering from the shock and trauma of an automobile accident which took place four years before my birth? I just tell them I have another flu affecting my stomach. They are used to me being sick.

As Heather turned away from her typewriter and slunk back to bed, she had no way of knowing she was only hours away from a magnificent breakthrough. Sleep came first, sheer exhaustion at last overwhelming her agitation. She slept until six o'clock that evening, groggily opening her eyes to the astonishing discovery that she was breathing comfortably without the aid of allergy pills! What's more, the habitual headache and ringing in the ears were gone. So was the usual constriction in the chest. Her skin, too, was clearer. At first she couldn't believe her good fortune. Neither could Dr Whitton as he listened to Heather's barely disguised ecstasy on the other end of the telephone line. When the allergies remained inactive after two more days free of medicinal encouragement, Heather ventured beyond her home environment to confront the untrust-

worthy gusts and crosscurrents of the outside world.
Her diary records the transformation:

Thursday, September 4, 1979: Saw K—— after my
singing lesson. I sat amid loads of cat fur, breathing in
her continuous cigarette smoke without as much as a
sneeze or a wheeze, and did not need an allergy pill
afterwards. This is unique for me and a great pleasure.

Tuesday, September 20, 1979: Saw Dr H—— today. I
had great difficulty explaining how I had suddenly lost
all my allergies. We both laughed a lot and she is delighted I am off allergy pills. The nurse remarked that
my skin has really improved.

While Heather was overjoyed at the apparent re-
treat of her allergies, she was subject for three weeks
to fits of crying, nightmares and depression.
Throughout this time she withdrew into her own
private world, shunning even the counsel of Dr Whitton who, not knowing what had been activated in
Heather's unconscious mind, preferred cautiousness
to optimism, even as he hoped that his patient's
dramatic improvement would not turn out to be a
temporary fluke. When Heather felt stable enough
to resume her weekly sessions, Dr Whitton wasted
no time in counting her down into trance. He wanted
to see this car accident for himself . . .

Isobel and a man called Robert are driving hard
towards the late afternoon sun that tilts splendidly
against the Mediterranean horizon. They are both nursing hangovers and arguing ferociously. Isobel is pregnant with Robert's child and wants to marry him;
Robert wants nothing of the kind. In his anger, Robert is
scorning the danger of hairpin bends along the sinuous

coast road that flanks the Maritime Alps near Juan Les Pins. At one of these bends the narrow road turns sharply northeast, but his Bugatti convertible is travelling too fast. The car crashes through a low roadside barrier, flies into the air, and bounces down the side of a cliff, uprooting small trees and bushes. There is a loud explosion as the vehicle smashes into a rocky outcrop. Robert is pinned behind the steering wheel and killed instantly. Isobel is thrown from the passenger seat into a patch of sandy soil where she lies unconscious. There are more explosions. Smoke and flame engulf Isobel's right side. Her dress and then her hair catch fire, the flames licking over the right side of her face . . .

The impact of the accident alone had been more than enough for Heather to contend with. Now she was horror-stricken all over again, transfixed by the unabridged drama just as an observer might have been. But she was also very much the victim of the crash, coughing and spluttering as Isobel's lungs were seared by the hot black smoke which poured from the burning car. Aware that she could withdraw from the hypnotic state any time she pleased, Heather watched the rescue effort that followed, noting the gathering crowd, the 'strange-looking squarish vehicles' that were the French fire tenders and the ambulance 'with a ringing bell, not a siren'. From a lower road, four orderlies bearing a stretcher scurried up the steep incline to where Isobel lay.

Heather wanted so much to avoid what was coming next. But it wasn't easy to avert her inner gaze now that she was burrowing into the seething core of her distress. The desire to look was irresistible . . .

Isobel is lying in a hospital room. Nurses in white uniforms are soaking large gauze bandages and placing them over parts of her red and blistered body ... She moans in pain. The entire right side of her body is badly burned. Her right eye and eyebrow disappear in swelling, oozing redness. The nurses keep applying sopping wet gauze, leaving it on for a few minutes, then carefully lifting it off. They are remarking that she must receive all the morphine she needs. They feel that their patient, whose embryonic child has been aborted in the accident, will die within twenty-four hours ...

Heather surfaced from the trance feeling physically sick, and Dr Whitton waited for several minutes before telling her that he believed she had penetrated to the heart of her allergy problem by re-experiencing the inhalation of fumes from the car wreck. Naturally Heather was overjoyed to be free of her allergies, but, even as she rejoiced at this development, the familiar 'rolling waves' of depression seemed to redouble in intensity. Moreover, the gruesome trance memories and the waves of despair seemed inextricably entwined.

As Heather laboured under the strain of aroused memory, she became more and more curious about Isobel, a curiosity she felt compelled to satisfy. Dr Whitton actively encouraged further past-life exploration, believing there was every chance that Isobel could also account for the depressions. For the next few weeks, each self-hypnotic trance that Heather embarked upon added to her knowledge of Isobel's life leading up to the car accident. The experiences were not always pleasurable. In fact, the more Heather learned about Isobel, the less enamoured she became with her immediate past-life personality ...

Beneath the delicate assurance of her piano playing, her affluent background, her charm, popularity and ravishing good looks, Isobel is afflicted by deep psychological problems. An exceptionally talented concert pianist, she has everything a young woman could wish for, and yet she is selfish and self-destructive and seemingly incapable of feeling, or understanding, real love. Perhaps this is because her childhood was devoid of affection. Orphaned at an early age, she is raised by a housekeeper envious of her wealth and beauty.

At nineteen years of age, Isobel crosses the Atlantic Ocean to study piano at a music school in New York City. The year is 1924. Her manager, a Russian Jew named Nickolaus, has booked several recitals for her in the United States. Soon after her arrival in America, however, Isobel's professional dedication begins to wane. She is distracted by the appeal of a socialite's butterfly lifestyle, and heavy drinking, parties and promiscuity take up more and more of her time.

When Isobel returns to England, she decides to marry Nickolaus who, being like a father to her, represents her only security. But her rakish way of life is by now well-established, and she continues to indulge in a succession of affairs, both in London and the south of France. Her sexual aimlessness expires only when she meets Robert at a Mediterranean yacht party. They return to London together and, discovering that she is carrying his child, Isobel wants to run away with him. This leads to a showdown with Nickolaus. While the couple are arguing, Isobel storms out of their London townhouse. Only later, some days after she has fled with Robert in the Bugatti, does Isobel learn that Nickolaus is dead and that their row provoked the massive heart attack that killed him . . .

Heather became increasingly aware that she had inherited much from Isobel in terms of predispositions as well as karmic debt. Growing up in Mexico City, Heather, too, played piano, had been told she possessed a 'genius' for the instrument, and had enrolled as a student at the finest music school in Mexico. Intriguing as it was to make such connections from one life to the next, there was much she would have preferred to forget, particularly the recurring image of Isobel's fire-ravaged body wrapped in gauze bandages. This oppressive vision begged the question: Did Isobel survive the car crash? The answer – produced in a succession of trances – prompted nightmares and sporadic weeping as she witnessed the grotesque descent of a gifted and beautiful soloist to a horribly maimed and suicidal woman isolated from the flamboyant society that had once succoured and adored her. The following is a condensation from Heather's diary of the most telling trance episodes:

In the winter of 1933 Isobel is living with a nurse and two servants in a seaside cottage near the town of Rye in Sussex, England. She moves very slowly and with a great deal of pain. Her vocal expression is limited to painful whispers. I force myself to take a close look at her – what a mess! Her face is scarred and distorted; the right eye and mouth are pulled askew. She is wearing a long silk scarf of a pale peach colour wound around her head and neck. Her right hand is covered with blisters and puckered skin and looks useless. There is a piano in the cottage, but Isobel's playing days are over. With her left hand she paints watercolours of flowers in a semi-realistic style.

Several times Isobel has thought about ending her wretchedness and these thoughts are inflamed by a visit from Eleanor, a fashionably overdressed 'friend' from

London. Eleanor sits on the couch sipping tea as she rubs her chatty conversation into Isobel's gaping wounds . . . 'Everybody keeps talking about your looks and hands having been ruined, Isobel dear. Of course, whenever they say anything nasty about you, I tell them how wrong they are. I don't think I could live if I were in your place. How can you stand it, my dear? I mean, how can you bear to look at yourself?' And so on.

Not long afterwards, Isobel walks out of the cottage into a howling winter's night. With sleet beating against her face, she crosses the field that separates her home from the shoreline and plods along beside a wrathful sea. Then she descends some slippery wooden steps to a beach of pebbles. Slowly and deliberately, she walks into the frigid and turbulent water and keeps on walking . . .

Heather's black moods were linked directly to this grim night when she last walked the earth as Isobel. After re-experiencing, in trance, the watery tomb of the English Channel, the rolling waves of depression never returned. To her amazement, Heather remembered writing a composition in which she had described Isobel's death scene in precise detail. As a schoolgirl, she had given full expression to her wildest thoughts and feelings, not caring how bizarre they might appear. 'You must be very unhappy,' her teacher had said. Taken as a criticism, this remark served to muzzle her desire to write creatively and repressed for years her apparently spontaneous memory of Isobel's suicide.

Now that the nature of Isobel's death had been revealed, Heather's remaining psychological problems became more and more apparent to Dr Whitton as he persevered in his search for further healing resonance. Under his guidance, Heather spent several weeks compiling an inventory of nineteen past lives which included a cave painter in the Dordogne, France, circa 13,000 BC; a craftsman in predynastic Egypt, circa 3,100 BC; a poverty-stricken artisan who lived in Changan, China, two centuries before the birth of Christ; a Roman woman who died in childbirth in the imperial province of Lusitania around AD 25; a twelfth-century Druid priestess from Brittany, France; and a French noblewoman who was cruelly put to death in late fifteenth-century Spain. Many of the lives showed Heather engaged in arts and crafts of some kind – appropriate precursors to the current incarnation. But none gave any intimation as to why she should be paralysed, in this life, by the very idea of artistic creation. And no reasons were revealed for her hypersensitivity and profound feelings of unworthiness.

Apart from Isobel's existence, the only life which appeared to have direct bearing on Heather's problems was the particularly ugly incarnation during the reign of Ferdinand II. Self-hypnosis revealed a French noblewoman named Evangeline journeying into Castile, where she met, fell in love with, and subsequently married a Spanish nobleman who was already betrothed to a woman Heather recognized as her mother in this life. An arch-rivalry developed between the two women, which culminated in a successful conspiracy against Evangeline involving the feared Office of the Inquisition. Heather's stomach rebelled as she transcribed the trance experience which recorded Evangeline's last hours in the dungeon of the Alcazar in Segovia, Spain:

Flashes of confusing scenes ebb away and I am left with the sight of flaming torches set into brackets in the dungeon walls. More light comes from a glowing brazier; brands and pincers are thrust into the coals. The smell of burning flesh hangs in the air. In a far corner, a dark-haired woman is talking to some burly men wearing hoods . . .

Evangeline is suspended by her wrists from iron cuffs attached by chains to the ceiling. Her arms look as though they have been pulled from her shoulder sockets; her head has fallen forward. She is stripped to the waist, and her skin is scorched and bruised. Her eyes have been burned out.

Evangeline's limp body is taken down, wrapped in burlap, and removed to a cell. Long after the cell door is secured, she starts to regain consciousness and, later still, rats appear and begin to gnaw at her body. Barely alive, she is unable to chase the rats away . . .

This scene left Heather in a state of upheaval. She wrote:

I was screaming in this trance and ready to throw up . . . Why is it that I seem to pick up all the effects of these scenes? I am having great difficulty typing. My arms feel limp and almost useless . . .

Heather's recognition of her mother as the 'dark-haired woman' in the dungeon galvanized Dr Whitton's interest, and he pressed for information on the mother–daughter relationship in this life. There was lots to give. Materially Heather's childhood had been a sumptuous and inexhaustible banquet. Emotionally, however, she was starved of affection and encouragement by an intensely jealous mother who, displaying an attitude of chilling resemblance to that of the jilted Spanish fiancée, saw her daughter as competition that must be beaten and demoralized. 'My mother hated me doing art more than anything else,' Heather remembers. This spirit of obstruction prevailed throughout childhood and continued into her university years. In her early forties, as Heather struggled with the worst phase of her degenerative illness, 'every discouraging word my mother had ever said came tumbling back. I felt I was unworthy and didn't deserve to be happy.'

At last details were emerging that were fundamental to the therapeutic consultation that was to follow. Dr Whitton was now almost certain that Heather's remaining psychological problems stemmed not from her past incarnations but from her unhappy childhood. And while he felt that orthodox therapy would relieve the symptoms that remained, he first wanted Heather to gain as many insights as possible into the meaning of her current life. That meant ushering her into the *bardo* that bridged the lives of Isobel and Heather. In earthbound terms, this between-life stay was brief – less than ten months separated Isobel's death in the winter of 1933 and Heather's birth in the summer of 1934. In a diary entry dated December 3, 1980, Heather described her sojourn in metaconsciousness, beginning with Isobel's surrender to the stormy English Channel:

I could see Isobel's body floating in a dark, broiling sea. There was a massive storm raging.

I knew that I had once been Isobel but now I didn't have a body. I was floating in all-embracing golden light. I felt comfortable and warm and untouched by the elements. Even though I didn't have a body I felt

*quite whole and at one with my surroundings. I realized
I could see in all directions.*

*Looking at Isobel's body, I felt no emotions. I felt no
fear and no loneliness, although I seemed to be alone.
Then the light spread and I appeared to be moving up.
I felt tremendous warmth and love and happiness. All
around me was golden light, as though I were basking
in very bright sunshine. There was no division, no
separateness. All was one. It was incredibly beautiful
and peaceful. I saw flashes of pastel rainbow hues and
heard hundreds of voices singing simple but beautiful
melodies. I just floated there happily, feeling I was a
part of it all, that I truly belonged.*

Heather was sorely tempted to remain adrift in this
delicious, light-filled boundlessness. But her need
for answers prevailed, and the bliss could not be
sustained as Isobel's karmic script was revealed. This
indicated a life that would have embraced a long and
brilliantly creative musical career had Isobel only
followed her chosen path. Recordings, concerts in
London and Paris, and a series of compositions were
all there, only awaiting the required effort in order
to be fulfilled. But Isobel, wandering far from her
interlife intentions, had flung open the door to chaos
and misery and squandered all prospect of rewarding
growth.

From what Heather could glean from the interlife,
her current life was hastily assembled as an emer-
gency measure; she was almost wrenched into being
to cope with the karmic repercussions of Isobel's
misspent and prematurely curtailed existence. Her
allergies, she learned, were more than a legacy of the
unresolved trauma of the car accident. Their role
was to provide the impetus that would force her to

make amends with her past. Of course, had Isobel
not been diverted by the prodigal life, Heather would
never have existed. 'I picked up from the interlife,'
she noted, 'that Isobel would have died just recently
as a happy, successful lady and great grandmother. If
only she had been patient and persevering, she could
have had it all.'

Nevertheless all the 'if onlys' and 'might have
beens' are of no practical consequence. Isobel's actions had created the very personification of her
karma – a new being called Heather who was also
equipped with a script detailing her intention to
grapple with the repercussions of past-life deeds.
Having been made aware in the interlife that she had
chosen to make reparation for Isobel's deficiencies,
Heather sought clarification on the major thrust of
her life's work. And this led to an electrifying encounter with members of the judgement board, who
revealed themselves at the far end of a vast temple.
The Three were in the guise of the Egyptian deities
Ra, Osiris and Isis . . .

> As I entered the temple, I picked up the rattle of the
> sistrum, which became more and more persistent. Also
> there was the sound of flutes and hand cymbals . . .
> beautiful and elusive at the same time.
> I walked forward straight to Isis. She was incredibly
> tall and communicated without words. She told me I
> must pursue my artistic endeavours, that as I worked
> I would find my answers . . .

The soul's glimpse of the forthcoming incarnation
as Heather was far from stimulating, however. All
the indications pointed to her experiencing a dismal
conglomerate of frustration, rejection and tears. Even

more disturbing was the unsolicited recommendation as to her best choice of womb. It was the last thing Heather wanted to hear . . .

> All of a sudden I felt horror and fear. I begged not to be born to my mother, but I received the impression that this was part of what I had to repay because of Isobel. I cannot describe my terror.
>
> Then I saw my grandmother, whom I recognized from a happier incarnation, and I started to feel a little better. I loved her and looked forward to seeing her again.

Like most voyages in metaconsciousness, this journey beyond the third dimension encompassed the full range of human emotions experienced at unforgettable levels of intensity. 'I almost screamed at the idea of rejoining my mother,' Heather said later. This ordeal brought on an acute attack of bronchial pneumonia that lasted several weeks. Once the illness ebbed away, she felt clearer, calmer and more optimistic, and her bronchial and pneumonic problems have never reappeared. The account in her diary for December 4, 1980, gives an almost audible sigh of relief:

> For the first time in a long time, I am actually starting to feel a little hope in this life. I feel that if I can ride out the storm, things will improve a little as I grow older. Already my life is slowly changing for the better, and I am starting to realize that people can like me. I even feel I might have a little artistic success if I can fight it through.

Over the next three years Dr Whitton helped Heather 'fight it through' by enabling her to come to terms with the negative influence that had wrecked her childhood and crippled her adult life. By means of systematic orthodox therapy *without* the aid of hypnosis she came to realize at the deepest level of her being that she is worthy of affection and respect. She was able to accept that her feelings of insecurity stemmed not from inherent inadequacy but, rather, from karmic demands that dealt the emotional punishment of her early years.

Gradually Heather grew less insecure and became less susceptible to the reactions of others. As her confidence grew, so did her ability to express herself. She felt more inclined to listen to others, whether or not their opinions were agreeable. Her husband, Philip, summed up the 'new' Heather when he said, 'She used to be terrified of her own shadow – not any more!'

This rejuvenation of the psyche – which attracted lots of friends – left Heather feeling liberated enough to channel renewed energy into photography as well as jewellery design. Her first gallery show was mounted soon after the final therapeutic session in 1983, and her skills are continuing to attract the interest of art dealers as well as private collectors.

In more ways than one, Heather Whiteholme is breathing much easier these days. Restored to a state of health and working capacity once only dreamed about, she pauses often to reflect on her past-life personalities, Isobel in particular. Heather now realizes that she has been thwarted in the expression of her abilities because Isobel dissipated rewards that were her birthright. With Dr Whitton's help, this frustration has been eliminated, enabling her to rebuild her life and renew her creative output. Back in 1979, a diary entry noted gloomily, 'I feel as though

I am wandering aimlessly through life without any meaning or purpose.' Metaconsciousness and past-life exploration changed all that. Now she's aware, daily, of attempting to resolve aspects of her personality that, having pushed Isobel to destruction, provide Heather with her very reason to be.

9

The Other Woman

> 'In love, ther is
> but litel reste.'
>
> *Geoffrey Chaucer,*
> *Troilus and Criseyde, IV*

Gary Pennington was perfectly content with married life. In a world where relationships seemed prone to breakdown and collapse, he marvelled at his own good fortune. His relationship with his wife, Elizabeth, had started in their teenage years when they were both attending the same Anglican church. Marriage followed as they pursued their respective university studies – he in psychology, she in English literature – and they soon settled into a relationship that was both mutually supportive and unusually resilient. In her early thirties, Elizabeth gave birth to a boy and then a girl, who were raised in a happy, relaxed household. Home was the ideal refuge for Gary, who, having earned his doctoral degree, was working for the legal system as a forensic psychologist assessing disturbed people charged with violent crimes. Gary lived for his wife and kids. In fact, the family's touching interdependence made them the envy of their friends, many of whose marital alliances had degenerated into separation and divorce.

After sixteen years of matrimony, Gary's passion for Elizabeth was undiminished, time having only enhanced her good looks and sensuality. Being well-suited to a staple emotional diet of hearth and home, Gary felt no hankering for an escape from family responsibilities. He hadn't even been seriously tempted by the occasional opportunity for sexual adventure. Yet when he very nearly collided with Caroline McVittie, at a pre-Christmas cocktail party in 1982, their exchange of glances left him feeling like a hot-blooded adolescent. Disturbed and yet strangely elated by this fleeting encounter, Gary wandered distractedly among the black ties and elegant dresses until he reached a line of bay windows hung with baskets of tropical plants.

Turning to face the crowded room, he knew that he *must* speak to the dark-haired woman who had thoroughly unsettled him. He scanned the guests until she appeared on the far side of the crush between the bar and the buffet table. She was looking his way as she chatted with an older woman in a green dress. Nervously Gary strode into the crowd, weaving past elbows, wine glasses and trays of *hors d'œuvres* until he was by her side. Although arrogant and self-confident by nature, he felt somewhat awkward as he introduced himself. But as they began to chat, his nervousness retreated in the face of instant affinity. 'It was like being welcomed home,' Gary would say later. Barely aware of the swirl of guests around them, they talked earnestly for the entire evening. And when the party was over, they both felt a compulsion to meet again . . .

The swiftness and intensity of the affair that developed between Gary and Caroline made heavy demands on their spare time. Yet Gary never attempted to conceal from his wife the reasons why he was spending less and less time at home. He told Elizabeth about the affair almost as soon as it began in expectation that she would be able to understand and tolerate his liaison with Caroline. Deeply hurt, Elizabeth couldn't and didn't want to understand, but for nearly three months she patiently withstood Gary's absences and did her best to cope with their growing estrangement. Elizabeth was miserable and she was angry. But most of all she was fearful. Inexplicably she had always been afraid that someday Gary would leave her. His affair only compounded these fears, turning them into tangible agents of terror.

One frosty Friday evening in March 1983, Elizabeth's quiet desperation broke cover. Gary returned home just after midnight to find her sprawled across their bed. At first he thought she had simply fallen asleep, but he changed his mind on walking into the bathroom to find a near-empty bottle of sleeping pills beside the basin. This discovery sent him rushing back into the bedroom where he attempted to rouse his wife by slapping her face and hands. Initially he was only partly successful, eliciting slight restlessness and a few muffled sighs. All the while, Gary's head thrummed with anxiety and self-torment as he was confronted with the obvious cause of Elizabeth's despair – himself. Shouldn't he call an ambulance? Of course, he answered himself, were it not for the complications that must surely follow. Through his work, Gary was known to just about every ambulance driver in the city. Elizabeth was bound to be embarrassed by the questioning of junior interns at the hospital, and his affair with its tragic coda would be the gossip of the medical-legal community.

Notwithstanding the vexation of this dilemma, Gary believed he would be able to prevent Elizabeth from falling into a coma. Every once in a while he shook her and rubbed her arms, but mainly he kept her talking until the first light of dawn stole through the bedroom blinds. Slowly, she managed to regain full consciousness. By then Gary had long made up his mind about Caroline, the other woman. The affair was well and truly over.

Caroline was devastated by Gary's hasty decision to break off their relationship. She reacted, shortly afterwards, by moving in with James Hughes, a wealthy bachelor in his early fifties with whom she lived for about three months. Then, apparently upset at his inability to commit himself to her, Caroline made a serious attempt at taking her own life. She rigged up a noose in the bathroom in imitation of a suicide sequence she had seen in the movie *An Officer and a Gentleman*. When Hughes returned home minutes later, he found her dangling from a rope knotted around the shower fixture. After cutting her down, he rushed her to a Toronto hospital, where she remained for almost two months. While Caroline's suicide bid appeared to be a direct consequence of Hughes' lack of romantic commitment, close friends – and even Hughes himself – maintained that the self-destructive urge sprang from deep but condemned passion for Gary. Hughes later contributed towards Caroline's recovery in a spectacular way. For more than a year, he paid for her to take weekly flights to New York for therapeutic sessions with an analyst. Why New York? Hughes didn't trust Toronto therapists because many of them were personally acquainted with Gary.

Gary Pennington's life was beginning to resume an even pace; his bruised marriage was healing with the passing of time. Elizabeth had done her best to forgive and forget, and accepted Gary's word that he was once more hers and hers alone. Gary for his part found he was able to forgive himself; the exploits of the lawbreakers he counselled rendered his extra-marital escapade a mere peccadillo in comparison. Besides, he was being won over by Bertrand Russell's oft-quoted passage in *Marriage and Morals*, which reads: 'The psychology of adultery has been falsified by conventional morals, which assume, in mono-gamous countries, that attraction to one person can-not coexist with a serious affection for another. Everybody knows that this is untrue.'

Gary could forgive himself easily enough. But he couldn't forget. Not only did he have to reconcile himself to the loss of Caroline and to his responsi-bility for her suicide attempt, but also he felt com-pelled to search for the reasons behind his uncharacteristic behaviour. Was there some flaw in his character? Was he depressed, or was some failing in his relationship with Elizabeth responsible for investing the romance with such irresistibility? There was another possible consideration. Could it be that the rapport he and Caroline felt for one another lay far beyond the vagaries of the here and now?

Gary was well aware of the concept of reincarnation, and as he brooded over the affair, he recalled a conversation in which a colleague had discussed Dr Whitton's interest in hypnotic regression. Being a highly respected professional whose counselling talents are well-recognized, Gary was naturally defensive about seeking the help of a psychiatrist, and for a long time he was apprehensive about making further enquiries. When at last he did seek out Dr Whitton, he was careful to explain that, because at least eight months had elapsed since the end of the affair, he was neither in distress nor in any hurry. Sooner or later, however, he wanted to know why he had flung himself so passionately into adultery.

Having thoroughly acquainted himself with Gary's personal and marital history, Dr Whitton felt that there was no ordinary psychological reason for the affair. Consequently he hypnotized his subject and instructed him to seek out any incarnations he may have shared with Caroline which could possibly explain their intimacy in this life. Gary's initial response to the trance state was both sudden and dramatic. Immediately he was transfixed by the roar of an aeroplane engine and the pungent smell of petroleum . . . he was Pilot Officer Peter Hargreaves standing beside an aircraft being prepared for takeoff from an airstrip near Salerno, Italy. The country was being ravaged by World War II and the presence of the Royal Air Force was vital to the success of the Allies' Italian Campaign. The year was 1944 . . .

Hargreaves is an RAF intelligence officer and not officially a pilot, although he has been trained to fly. Perturbed by aerial photographs which indicate mass-

ive preparations for a German counter-attack, he wants to learn more by inspecting the area in question from a low-flying plane. He is eager to be airborne in an unarmed Mustang P–51, but some fellow officers are remonstrating with him. They are telling him the mission is reckless and foolhardy, that confirmation should be left to air reconnaissance personnel.

Shrugging off their protestations, Hargreaves climbs into the cockpit and takes off. But as he closes in on the target zone, his plane is intercepted by German fighter aircraft. Bullets thud into the fuselage of his single-engine plane, one of these tearing into his left leg. This leaves him without full control of the foot pedals, and he is forced to crash-land in a field. He is captured and taken north by train to an SS interrogation centre where his shattered leg is left untended and becomes gangrenous. In a small, bare room, Hargreaves is beaten repeatedly with the intent of forcing him to reveal information about Allied operations. But despite the most extreme abuse, which deprives him of food, sleep and medical attention, he discloses nothing of value to the enemy. His heroism is rewarded by an agonizing death. In a final effort to extort military secrets, as he lay dying, his Nazi torturers resort to pulling out his fingernails . . .

Gary rebounded from trance severely shaken. In the hypnotic state, he was spared Hargreaves' physical suffering, but he felt keenly the doomed officer's despair and desolation. Having no conscious knowledge of the last war's Italian Campaign, Gary was at first inclined to doubt the veracity of the experience because his trance was scattered with references to Monte Cassino. 'Is this for real?' he asked Dr Whitton. 'What is a gambling joint doing in the middle of the war?' Gary had no idea that Monte Cassino, a huge Benedictine monastery commanding the entrance to the Liri valley, gave its name to the biggest battle of the campaign. In February 1944 the monastery was pummelled into ruins by six hundred tons of bombs as the Allies marched on Rome . . .

Gary left Dr Whitton's office that day in March 1984 with his mind racing. Scanning his life, he realized there was a coherence to formerly inexplicable experiences and inclinations. His trance explained an unforgettable flash of horror that had commandeered his senses at sixteen years of age, shortly before he met Elizabeth. This brief but startling vision – which appeared as he was enjoying himself at a party – had transported him to a bare room, where his nails were being pulled out by a well-dressed officer in Nazi uniform. Having just passed his driving test when the flashback occurred, Gary now wondered whether working the foot pedals of an automobile could, subconsciously, have recalled Peter Hargreaves' struggle with the aeroplane pedals, thus precipitating the torture scene. The revived memory set Gary wandering deeper into his past to recall that although he was born and raised in Canada, as a young child he used to speak with a British accent. This deceived his teachers into thinking that he was adopted. And while the accent soon faded, its very existence had remained a mystery . . . until now.

The trance episode explained Gary's lifelong phobia about breaking his leg, which had always held him back from taking up such hazardous sports as downhill skiing. It also accounted for his unwarranted anxiety about travelling by aeroplane. Wishing to confront this apprehension, he toyed with the idea of gaining his pilot's licence, feeling instinctively that he already knew how to fly a small plane. It was only a fear of being reckless – a fear he now well understood – that restrained him. This recklessness remains very much a part of Gary's nature, a trait that has led him to have several brushes with death, notably while driving.

Gary then began to reflect upon the resemblance of his own work to intelligence gathering; forensic psychology logically succeeded his past-life vocation. Furthermore he better understood why he was now an inveterate nail-biter and why he harboured an almost perverse fascination with torture. Gary had been granted more self-awareness than he had dared to hope for, but he had yet to be enlightened about his adulterous behaviour. The next session enlarged upon his immediate past life and, in so doing, brought him face to face with the other woman . . .

Peter Hargreaves has been raised in an upper middle class English Catholic home by an Italian nanny. His fluency in the Italian language is one of the main reasons he is called on to liaise with the local resistance fighters as the Allies gain a foothold on mainland Italy. In Salerno, his main contact with the resistance movement is a young woman called Elena Bocchi, who enables him to communicate with partisans in the mountainous hinterland. From the outset, Hargreaves and Elena are strongly attracted to one another, and they fall in love as they work together under the most harrowing conditions. Elena's father has recently been killed in combat, and Hargreaves steps in to provide as best he can for the destitute Bocchi family. He promises to marry her as soon as the war is over.

Hargreaves, as we have seen, did not survive the

war. However, his brutal treatment by the Nazis and his love and concern for Elena detained him on the earth plane for several weeks after his death. On his first visit to the between-life state, Gary found his past-life personality still earthbound and over-wrought with emotion, particularly anger. Meta-consciousness revealed that Hargreaves had been shot down because a Nazi agent had infiltrated the partisans and alerted the Germans to his intended escapade in the single-engine plane. Furious, Har-greaves' discarnate self kept replaying the circum-stances of the betrayal.

Elena learned of Hargreaves' death through under-ground connections. Watching from the life between life, Hargreaves perceived her extreme dismay, which developed quickly into a deep and lasting depression . . .

> With mounting apprehension, he watches Elena pro-ceed to a clifftop near Salerno, determined to commit suicide. When she reaches the edge, Hargreaves' discar-nate self tries desperately to materialize in order to prevent her from killing herself. 'If only I had a body,' his mind keeps repeating, 'this need never happen.' Thoroughly frustrated with his disembodied state, he can do no other than look on as Elena leaps to her death.

(Hargreaves' fruitless efforts to prevent his lover's suicide did not go unnoticed. Caroline – who has recalled several past lives through meditation – has a final memory from her immediate past life that corresponds precisely to Gary's trance account. She remembers struggling with an invisible force before throwing herself over the cliff.)

Having failed to avert Elena's suicide, Hargreaves'

disembodied consciousness returned to the scene of his agony in the SS interrogation centre. There too he tried to intervene but was unsuccessful in preventing the torture of those prisoners who survived him. While still angry at being betrayed, he felt guilty about his unfulfilled promises to Elena and tormented himself for his inability to prevent her death. He also felt horribly inadequate in failing to stop the persecution of those languishing in the interrogation centre. Only when he was approached by a wise and elderly being, presumably a guide, did he agree to surrender his earthbound attachment. With great reluctance, he left the tragic circumstances of Hargreaves' life.

Gary's attraction to Caroline had been accounted for by Peter Hargreaves' love affair with Elena Bocchi, but their association went deeper still. Dr Whitton assisted Gary in finding a Russian life in which he lived with his younger sister in an incestuous relationship. Seeing himself as a somewhat portly figure named Sevastjan Umnov, Gary identified Caroline as Sevastjan's sister, Lisenka.

Sevastjan is an emissary of Czarina Elizabeth Petrovna to the court of Louis XV during the mid-eighteenth century. Because relations between France and Russia are capricious, his major diplomatic responsibilities are similar to those of a secret agent, and he specializes in counter-intelligence operations and in arranging arms exports to his homeland.

The demands of diplomacy require Sevastjan to be away from Lisenka for long periods of time. Being deeply in love with him, she worries constantly that her brother is involving himself with other women in Paris or Versailles. Her jealousy is unfounded, but, on hearing a *particularly disquieting rumour about her brother's behaviour, she reacts impetuously by marrying an admiring acquaintance. Only a few weeks later, she hangs herself in despair at having denied herself all hope of continuing the relationship she treasures most. Sevastjan is heartbroken when the news reaches him in France, and he never again returns to Russia. He dies of natural causes, alone and unhappy . . .*

It might have been coincidental that Gary and Caroline were dining at a Russian restaurant the night Elizabeth swallowed the sleeping pills. But Gary had less and less faith in coincidence, choosing to accept, in the words of Walter Pater, that 'taste is the memory of a culture once known'. In the light of reincarnational experience, everything seemed to be charged with new meaning. Gary's trances reflected the self and its actions and reactions like a hall of mirrors. Two major themes were revealed – the incorporation of similar skills and abilities in Gary's working lives and Caroline's penchant for suicide which, as reincarnation investigators such as Dr Ian Stevenson have shown, can exert a domino effect from life to life. Given their past-life history, it was now clear why Gary and Caroline should have come to participate in yet another relationship. But this understanding led to even more pressing questions about Gary's marriage. Had he and Elizabeth also reunited after sharing other lives? The next trance session, which showed Gary to be Jeremy Everett, a nineteenth-century mathematics lecturer at Oxford University, answered strongly in the affirmative . . .

For years Jeremy has been leading a double life. On

weekends he breaks away from his lectures and tu-
torials to rejoin his wife and two young sons at their
home in Oxford's neighbouring countryside. During the
week, however, Jeremy lives on the university campus.
Nearby he keeps a mistress who has two infant daugh-
ters. Jeremy has fathered these children and has pro-
mised repeatedly to take good care of them and to
ensure that they are well-educated. It's a pledge that
will never be fulfilled, for, in his late thirties, Jeremy
develops pneumonia and dies unexpectedly, leaving
two dependent families. His wife is well looked after.
She has received the ownership of the family property,
miscellaneous assets, and a small personal inheritance.
But his mistress and her children are not nearly so
fortunate. Jeremy, still young and lacking foresight, has
failed to make enduring provision for them. Full of
rancour at her lover's demise, the mistress blames him
for the extremely difficult and impecunious circum-
stances that ensue ...

Gary's wife in this English incarnation is unknown
to him today. But the trance state revealed that his
current wife and the mistress whom he abandoned
through death are unmistakably one and the same.
Elizabeth has exchanged roles – a hallmark of the
phenomenon of group reincarnation. Gary went on
to learn that he and Elizabeth had shared several
previous lives as secret lovers. Indeed, the present
life appeared to be the first time that their relationship has been enjoyed openly. Further hypnotic regression revealed a life in ancient Egypt when
Elizabeth, prized for her ornamental value, was a
consort to Pharaoh Amenhotep III; Gary, meanwhile,
was captain of the palace guard. A clandestine affair
developed between them, only for Elizabeth to

lose her lover when Gary was killed in a brawl. Under these circumstances, it is little wonder that Elizabeth has always feared her husband would leave her; precedents had been set in earlier existences.

The past-life reasons for Gary's own fears were progressively being enlarged upon. Because of his unfulfilled promises to the mistress in England, he was able to understand his exaggerated anxiety regarding the financial security of his family. His greatest fear of all was that he would not be able to provide adequately for his wife and children. Now he knew why he had felt driven to sign up for large amounts of life insurance just in case he should suffer a fatal accident.

When Gary returned to the *bardo*, bridging the death of Peter Hargreaves in 1944 and his own birth some two years later, he received the strong impression that the emotional momentum from previous lives had once more pitched Elizabeth, Caroline and himself into the task of refining their natures through intense interaction. As Gary was about to meet the judgement board, he became aware of the sensation that had he possessed a body, that body would have had no fingers – clearly a throwback to his treatment by the Nazis. He perceived the Three as idealized forms of Jesus Christ, a representation that most probably can be traced to Hargreaves' Catholic background.

Gary felt strongly that these adjudicators were well-acquainted with his soul-identity and, as the review of Peter Hargreaves' life proceeded, he was aware of the missing fingers being returned to his 'shadow' body. This, he believed, symbolized that he had been forgiven – or more precisely, had forgiven himself – for the recklessness which had led to his premature death. The Three cautioned him about his characteristic foolhardiness that had reached across several incarnations and warned him not to get involved in another military career until the tendency had been controlled. (During the early 1970s, Gary wanted to join the US Army in Viet Nam as an intelligence officer. But he was dissuaded from this idea by the insistent promptings of an inner voice.) The Three also told him that the pride he held in his knowledge and intellectual ability must give way to humility; he must become not weak, but meek.

In this life, Gary is still grappling with innate recklessness, pride in his abilities – which often surfaces as arrogance – and a susceptibility to betrayal in both personal and professional situations. This latter theme was not addressed by the judgement board, but it appears that his soul's anger at being betrayed was so incorrigible during the interlife that Gary has carried his negativity back into this incarnation. Consequently he has difficulty trusting even those who are close to him – including his elder brother, Graham. Shortly after Gary and Caroline started their affair, Elizabeth confided in Graham and asked for his help in restoring the equilibrium of their marriage. Graham then invited his brother out to dinner, and Gary looked forward to the opportunity to voice his most personal feelings to a sympathetic listener. But Graham, acting as Elizabeth's agent, condemned his behaviour. Gary was deeply wounded by this reaction.

Four months of hypnotic sessions provided Gary

with a greater awareness of his own situation as well as a broader understanding of the motivations that underlie human behaviour. Before journeying into past lives and metaconsciousness, he tended to be harshly judgemental. Now, mindful of the unseen influence of karmic forces, he shows greater tolerance towards himself and others.

In his own mind, Gary has thoroughly resolved the reasons for the affair which ended not only as a result of Elizabeth's desperate protest but also because Gary and Caroline were being constantly challenged by circumstances. Emotional momentum brought them together, but the absence of interlife planning – the glue of relationships – decreed that they had no future together in this incarnation. 'It felt as though we were two actors who simply ran out of lines,' said Gary. His relationship with Elizabeth, on the other hand, can be likened to a duet that, although briefly interrupted by a third voice, is expected to continue until curtain call.

Gary's karmic case study raises a monumental question about the nature of all romantic involvement. As long ago as 1953, the celebrated sex researcher Alfred Kinsey reported that in the United States, approximately half of married men and a quarter of married women participate in at least one extramarital affair during their lifetimes. Most partnerships of this kind arise from marital boredom invaded by compelling sexual attraction to a person who is conventionally 'out-of-bounds'. The genesis of such liaisons usually ensures their early collapse, the affairs foundering when initial passion subsides. But there are other affairs in which powerful emotions join forces with sexual magnetism to create an adulterous relationship of genuine affection. Gary's hypnotic experiences suggest that intimacy in other lives may be one of the most important factors in the awakening, or reawakening, of these emotions.

10

Sharp
Illumination

'. . . the world's mine oyster,
Which I with sword will open.'

William Shakespeare,
The Merry Wives of Windsor

Recoiling in horror on Dr Whitton's red leather couch, Linda Irving watched the long, curved blade being thrust into her side. She noticed that her assailant was masked, and she admired the craftsmanship of the silvery steel as it pierced her ribcage and sliced through her intestines. Then she was screaming awful, guttural screams. Only *she* wasn't screaming and *she* wasn't dying . . . *he* was, this heavy-bodied man who shared her identity, this killer named Rudolf Meyer who deserved to die in the Paris prison they called Conciergerie. It was a cool, damp evening in the year 1761 . . .

The being that watched Rudolf slump to the dirt floor of his cell was neither Linda nor Rudolf and yet embraced both of them. Through the agency of this disembodied self, Linda viewed the murderer's flight through the gloomy passageways of the prison. For a while, she hovered high over Rudolf's corpse, noticing the specks of torchlight beyond the high, barred windows that stretched the length of the cell block. Then she heard a voice, Dr Whitton's voice, coaxing her to leave Rudolf behind. 'Go further,' he murmured. 'What do you see?'

Suddenly, gloriously, the darkness was blanked out by intense brightness as Linda found herself being sucked through a pulsating, light-filled tunnel. All cares and fears were left behind. Space and time were no more than a memory. Linda was totally at peace with herself and at one with engulfing beauty and serenity as she emerged from the tunnel into an ineffable light-filled vastness. She felt she had come home.

Once she became acclimatized to these bright surroundings, Linda found herself in a marble square which radiated the same intense brightness that had marked her journey so far. Three of the corners were occupied by beings she identified as her judges. And when she took her place in the remaining corner, she found she was able to review with the utmost objectivity the life that had just ended.

'Speak!' the judges commanded in unison. Linda responded by telling the board of judgement that she knew she deserved to die violently. The judges agreed with this evaluation and told her that her actions as Rudolf would mean prolonged suffering in the life to follow as Maria Tovar. In the life after her next life, however, the Three indicated that while incarnate as Linda Irving she would 'look at what went wrong and mend it'.

In this life, Linda is a petite, soft-spoken thirty-year-old, gently purposeful in her disposition. She's a strict vegetarian, avoids caffeine and alcohol, practises yoga and meditation and, in her spare time, paints watercolours and teaches ballroom dancing. But most of all her life is her work as an occupational therapist. While attending high school in Detroit, Linda had set her mind on a career in the healing arts. After moving to Canada, she decided to study occupational therapy at the University of Toronto and, once she had graduated, began to practise at a hospital in the city's west end.

Instinct and intuition had drawn Linda to a career in which she helps those who have suffered from accident or illness to overcome physical, mental and emotional disabilities. But only by experiencing journey after journey into past lives and the life between lives could she discover the reason for such inner compulsions. Moreover, repeated hypnotic excursions would allow her to overthrow irregular, enervating depressions and a 'block' that seemed to thwart every attempt to realize her full potential. Through metaconsciousness, the meaning and purpose of Linda's life became almost tangible. Linda's karmic case study starts long before her encounter with Rudolf Meyer, when life wasn't quite so sweet . . .

In November 1983, acting on the recommendation of a friend, Linda contacted Dr Whitton in the hope that past-life exploration would be able to alleviate problems that had refused to go away. Although she didn't feel that these problems were related to her childhood, Linda had endured a difficult upbringing. For as long as she could remember, her father had been suicidal, and his desperation frequently pushed her parents to the brink of breakup. Linda, however, possessed an intuitive understanding of her father's problems, and she was able, in times of crisis, to hold the family together. She was strengthened rather than debilitated by the challenges and upsets of her early years. Being extremely self-analytical by nature, she spent her teenage years coming to terms with the trying environment at home.

By her mid-twenties, Linda felt she had managed this accommodation successfully except that she couldn't shake off the periodic depressions that enveloped her, smothering her initiative and natural well-being. Linked with these depressions was the sense that she was somehow being blocked from fulfilling her true nature. 'I had the distinct impression,' said Linda, 'that I had brought this limitation with me into this life and that I couldn't make any more progress until it had been removed.' This emotional barricade caused trouble in a variety of ways – its presence curtailed her ability to be open and loving towards others, made her apprehensive of speaking in public, and left her feeling 'not myself' in personal relationships. She found herself grappling with one more psychological problem: a chronic fear of making a serious mistake. This phobia led to passivity and inertia, and reinforced the feeling of being held back by an invisible force.

Believing in reincarnation, Linda didn't need to be convinced of the reality of past lives. But during the first two sessions with Dr Whitton, she felt that her imagination might have been responsible for the maelstrom of images that swirled around a castle somewhere in medieval England. She saw herself as

John, a castle guard dressed in a brown, yellow and blue tunic. Then – seemingly out of nowhere – the date 1842 flashed on to the screen of her mind. Unquestionably out of time, thought Linda. But the medieval images kept flitting by until suddenly they were more than images. They were actual happenings, very much of the present moment, and Linda was forgotten as John ran after a horse-drawn cart, panting and yelling for it to stop. It wouldn't stop . . . Linda returned to normal consciousness, well and truly initiated in the mysteries of past-life experience.

Having instructed Linda to search for the source of her block, Dr Whitton felt that the sudden appearance of the year 1842 into an obviously anachronistic setting indicated a tactic of avoidance on the part of her subconscious mind. All he could do was press on, trusting that any reluctance to examine unsavoury past-life events would be overcome. His diligence was soon rewarded. When Linda next entered the hypnotic state, she found herself in the body of a seventeen-year-old woman who was dancing enthusiastically to Spanish music in a Madrid ballroom. As her head moved from side to side in time to the fast-paced music, the embroidered pattern decorating the hem of her dress swirled before her eyes, a pattern that progressively filled her trance vision until every stitch was visible. Linda felt herself pass through the pattern and into the ballroom. She understood the year to be 1842, and this time it *felt* like 1842 as she became Maria Tovar, the daughter of a wealthy merchant. She was dancing spiritedly and flirtatiously with Carlos Baroja, a strikingly handsome young man about the same age as herself.

'Move to an event that has great significance for the current lifetime,' prompted Dr Whitton.

Captivated by her own enjoyment and Carlos' dashing companionship, she didn't want to leave the ballroom. Neither did she want to see what Dr Whitton wanted her to see, for in responding to his command, Linda sank into a swamp of sorrow: the vivacious young woman of twelve years earlier had been superseded by a stolid, grief-stricken widow. Maria, dressed entirely in black, was mourning the death of Carlos, her army officer husband, who had just been killed during the Spanish revolution of 1854. Beside her stood their children – Fernando and Jorge, six-year-old twins, and a daughter, Katarina, age three, whom she especially loved. Her despair was asphyxiating in its intensity.

This was no temporary affliction. As Linda was moved through Maria's life, she felt only deepening depression and self-pity. Some fourteen years after Carlos' death, Fernando and Jorge marched off in the name of queen and country to fight another rebellion, never to return. Then Katarina married and moved away from home. Maria withdrew from the world into a grand house on a main street in Madrid which she shared, somewhat resentfully, with her mother-in-law. She nurtured her bitterness like a rare and prized flower.

Ushered forward to the last day of Maria's life, Linda found herself at forty-five pacing restlessly through the sepulchral home while drums and shouting and marching feet reverberated in the street outside. On January 29, 1984, Linda sat down and wrote in her diary about Maria's state of mind during these final, fateful hours . . .

I hate my house, this house that could have been, should have been, *our* house. This empty house that should have been full. Sometimes I hate Carlos and my children for leaving, especially Katarina, who had had a choice in the matter. But it's easier to hate that which remains. I hate the dark, empty house. And I hate myself. The more time I spend in the house, the more like it I become.

How I crave light! But the window that leads onto the street below sheds no light at all, only another horrifying glimpse of human blindness. Another parade for yet another leader. The leaders keep changing and each one leads in darkness, and the soldiers out there in the street all follow in blindness. Why don't they understand that this leader will take them to the same death as all the others?

I would change it if I could. But what am I? Dark, empty, hopeless Maria. I, too, should join them in that street of despair. I cannot bear the darkness any longer . . .

In Dr Whitton's office, the recall of Maria's memories had been so vivid that it was as if Linda were staring through Maria's eyes. She remained motionless for some time looking at the second-floor window that overlooked the noisy street. Then she was aware of a shaft of light that began just beyond the open shutters and, beguiled by its brilliance, she walked towards the window, towards the light . . . The street rushed up to meet her and she felt its numbing impact followed by the wheels of a horse-drawn carriage crushing her chest. But she was also aware, from a higher perspective, of her body sprawled across the cobbles, pinned between a criss-cross of wheel spokes. How inconsequential was this mortal husk now that the blinding light was forcing her attention upwards, away from the street. The street didn't matter. She had walked into the light, a light more lustrous and dazzling than the sun yet devoid of any sensation of heat. This absorbing brightness exuded peace and serenity and, utterly relaxed, she basked in its benevolence. There was also the impression of being enclosed in a tunnel or tube or cocoon. Words were quite unequal to the task of describing the magnificent environment through which she was drawn at incredible speed . . .

'Who are you?' asked Dr Whitton.

Linda wasn't sure. Confusedly the names Maria and Linda both came to mind and yet neither seemed particularly appropriate.

'Where are you?'

All that seemed to matter was the brightness and the serenity and Dr Whitton's voice sounded so irrelevant, so extraneous that, although wanting to reply, Linda felt no compunction to answer. It was all she could do to assimilate the wondrous atmospherics of this landscape without terrain as, slowly, she began to establish her whereabouts . . . Linda's diary for February 5, 1984, tells more:

What was this place? I needed time to adjust. Eventually some of the shock of my transition wore off and I began to be conscious of emotions. The sadness was so intense I wanted to cry. There was nothing else to do. Tears welled up, but there was that voice again . . . I told Dr Whitton that Maria's suffering was unfair. It was as if I were defending myself, but I had to justify Maria and her last act.

Maria hadn't thought about an afterlife. Yet it made sense that I should still be conscious after the death of the body. This was where I was. This was what was. It was beautiful, marvellous. I didn't want to leave . . .

No matter how timeless the interlife may be, explorations in metaconsciousness are limited: Dr Whitton's busy schedule necessitated Linda's return to mundane reality. Few return from the interlife without undergoing an aftermath of readjustment. Linda's diary describes how, after this sojourn in the life between lives as Maria Baroja and Linda Irving, she returned home and fell asleep for two hours despite the loud persistence of her roommate's bongo drumming! She then found herself unable to function normally for the rest of the day and was deprived of her usual alertness for a full week. Long, deep sleeps and low energy levels were her daily fare as she sensed, somewhere in the depths of her being, the warring demands that precede psychological transformation. Through it all, the bliss of metaconsciousness was often recalled. 'I have thought of that bright world with some longing,' she noted. 'I am glad I can go back there in memory because it will be a while before I can leave Linda behind.' Linda returned to the *bardo* in memory many times over the next few days, less to revel in remembered transcendence than to search for practical illumination. Mulling over the life between life gave her the first intimations that Maria's despair, while flowing ostensibly from the death of Carlos, may not have been quite so unfair after all . . .

When Linda returned to the interlife during her next session, she was intent on learning more about Maria's pain. Her diary entry for March 6, 1984, reports:

Looking at Maria from the vantage point of the inter-life I saw that she was selfish, caring only for her own welfare and her own need of love and companionship. I saw also that she had blocked herself from meeting these needs. She was not so much mourning the death of Carlos and her two sons but, instead, was grieving at her own loss. After the death of Carlos, she could have turned her grief to positive account by using it to deepen her empathy and strengthen the bonds with her children. But she refused to allow any light to enter her life and made only feeble efforts to overcome her grief and be a loving mother. The deaths of her two sons were less of a loss to her than a confirmation of the pain instigated by Carlos' death. By focusing even more on that pain, she undermined her relationship with her daughter, Katarina. Maria's selfishness is apparent in her reaction to Katarina's marriage – she felt no joy for her daughter, only more sadness and desolation for herself.

This knowledge was vital. But, as usual, there was more to learn. Dr Whitton wanted her to discern from the interlife how, specifically, Maria's life and death had influenced Linda's own incarnation. In response to careful probing, Linda had a vision of her oversoul as a cabbage of light with a dark mass of primeval sadness at its core. She saw that with each incarnation the cabbage unfolds a new leaf of light in order to release a few particles of darkness and shed some of the pain. After the growth of many leaves or lives, the cabbage manages to expunge all pain and is suffused with effulgence.

The cabbage was Linda's personal symbol for soul development. Her lives were seen to be as seemingly endless as the leaves of the cabbage in contrast to the rose which dies soon after its petals are opened.

Thus it became apparent that Maria, by dwelling on her pain and grief to the exclusion of all else, had allowed her life, or cabbage leaf, to become stunted by blinding herself to the potential for growth. This failure of hers was carried into the succeeding incarnation to provoke Linda's depressions and the 'block' that stood in the way of personal fulfilment.

Recognizing this, Linda felt the first delicious ripples of liberation. Though her life had not been nearly so traumatic as Maria's, the similarity of her attitudes to those of her immediate past-life personality was shocking to behold. She too had allowed herself to be trapped in a self-defeating state of depression. This gloom, this 'block', was Maria's heirloom to Linda, who in becoming aware of the pattern of self-perpetuation realized she was able to throw off its inhibiting influence. With understanding came freedom . . .

Linda's first act of freedom was to telephone her ex-boyfriend whom she had been pining for ever since his marriage two years' earlier. For two hours they chatted animatedly across the 540 miles that separate Toronto from Montreal and afterwards Linda knew that her waiting days were over. She had been released from pointless longing. Said Linda, 'Just as Maria waited for Carlos to return long after his death, my tendency had been similarly unrealistic – to hang on in spite of the pain. Only after my second visit to the interlife could I truly accept that, acting in this way, I was preventing myself from having a worthwhile relationship with someone else.'

Over the next few weeks, bubbles of illumination

arose from Linda's experiences in metaconsciousness to drift, at intervals, into her waking mind. She came to understand, for example, that her extraordinary sympathy for her father and his suicidal tendencies stemmed from her incarnation as Maria. Most important of all, her diary shows that she was beginning to enjoy herself . . .

March 14, 1984: For the last few days I have been feeling as though I've made a breakthrough. My energy is flowing so much more freely this week . . . The block is starting to dissolve. How much happier is this life than my last one! So much more progress . . .

April 8, 1984: I think I have now worked through most of Maria's problems. I feel lighter, clearer. I am more 'me'. The intense depressions have lifted . . .

Linda's new-found gaiety was evident to all who knew her. No longer debilitated by clinging negativity, she was able to be more giving and more receptive. The image of the shining cabbage would reappear over and over again, quietly exhorting her 'to radiate as much light as possible'. Only one problem remained: she was still disturbed by a chronic fear of making a terrible mistake.

Dreams can be pointers to past-life experience, and it was a particularly vivid dream on the night of May 15, 1984, that hinted at the resolution of this final problem. In the dream, a friend appeared to Linda and said, 'I am going to show you something from a past life,' whereupon Linda felt herself roll over on her left side and turn into a man. This man was in prison and he was screaming loudly from a deep stab wound inflicted in his right side by a sword like an elongated sickle. At the point of his death, the stream of images came to a temporary halt. When the pause ended, Linda was screaming again, only this time she was a tiny baby girl. Despite having just been born, she knew she was screaming at the memory of the stabbing.

Linda told Dr Whitton of the dream and explained that she considered its imagery a deliberate attempt by her subconscious mind to nudge a significant past-life episode into conscious awareness. Dr Whitton concurred and instructed Linda, under hypnosis, to locate this life and explore its relevance to her present circumstances. Quickly Linda snapped back into a rerun of the stabbing scene from her dream. She was a prisoner called Rudolf Meyer watching the shiny blade enter her side, knowing that this violent death was exactly what she deserved. Then she left the sinister mood of the death scene to become Rudolf at twelve years of age. The young Rudolf, overjoyed at the sight of flowers and butterflies, romped through a field of tall grass on a farm in Germany somewhere near the Swiss border. 'I had a sense,' Linda said later, 'that I was enjoying my last moments of innocence.'

When Dr Whitton asked Linda to leave the boy Rudolf behind and move forward ten years, he was confronted by an altogether different human being. Rudolf at twenty-two was an aggressive, cynical student at a Paris university. He spoke guardedly about being a member of a secret club of thirteen men. Dr Whitton's repeated requests for the club's name were sternly rebuffed, but Rudolf did reveal that social activism in pre-revolutionary France was the avowed aim of the group. And he admitted, somewhat proudly, that the organization 'scares political leaders by threatening them'.

'Are you terrorists?' asked Dr Whitton.

'We don't think so,' Rudolf replied with a gruff French accent, 'but others see us that way. Our methods are not always acceptable, but the ends are good.'

Dr Whitton instructed Linda to move forward one year to the age of twenty-three. Suddenly Rudolf became fretful, agitated . . .

Members of the club are disappearing one by one and nobody knows how or why this is happening. There are rumours about a beautiful redhead called Henriette who, being married to a club member, has learned of the revolutionaries' clandestine activities. She had wanted to join the club but has been rejected because she is a woman. Nevertheless several members are infatuated with her and the disappearances lead Rudolf to suspect that Henriette is vengefully seducing and then killing each man. But it is only when Rudolf's best friend, Jan, dies in suspicious circumstances that, in his own words, Rudolf becomes 'crazy' enough to plan Henriette's murder. 'She is evil – like a witch,' Rudolf tells Dr Whitton. 'I must stop her from killing more men.'

In the next trance session, Linda discovered Rudolf in jail trying gamely to suppress the vile act that had put him there. How hard he worked at dodging and resisting Dr Whitton's questions! As Linda strove to break through Rudolf's reluctance, she found her vision was obstructed by flames, always flames. At last, however, she saw herself in Rudolf's powerful body pushing a woman with long red hair into a fire.

She could smell the pungent stench of burning flesh.

> Dr Whitton: Why are you doing this?
> Linda (grimacing): *Don't ask me now. It's hard enough for me to go through with it.*
> Dr Whitton (insistently): Why are you doing this?
> Linda: *I hate her. She's part of a plan.*
> Dr Whitton: What plan?
> Linda: *Someone will smell the flesh . . . I must escape.*

After forcing Henriette into the fire and having watched the flames subdue her screams, Rudolf does not remain a free man for long. He is captured and brought in chains to the Conciergerie where, day after day, he sits and watches the burning woman dance on the walls of his cell. Remorse plagues every waking moment until Henriette's brother takes revenge by arranging his murder. Linda's voice is a tearful whimper as she tells Dr Whitton: 'I had to stop her from killing more men, but I should have been able to do that without killing her too. It was . . . a terrible mistake.'

Linda remained in the grip of guilt as she walked away from this hypnotic session, and Dr Whitton knew that her pent-up emotion would soon find release. Expressionless, she managed to hold herself in check until she had almost reached home. Then, rushing into the house, she flung herself on her bed crying, 'I killed her!' with an intensity that surprised even Linda. It wasn't until several hours later, when her body was weak from prolonged sobbing, that she became aware of a distinct adjustment to her psychological state. Linda was no longer haunted by the fear of committing a serious mistake.

The mistake that had made Linda anxious was

Rudolf's tragic error. Only now could she appreciate that Rudolf's self-reproach had been brought forward into the life of today as fear of repetition. It was no longer necessary. On July 26, 1984, she wrote in her diary:

> Ever since my life as Rudolf, I have been punishing myself. I felt I deserved to be murdered in prison. Then, as Maria, I made myself suffer by living like a dead woman. In this life, I was almost following in Maria's footsteps . . .

Just as Rudolf appeared to be the source of Linda's problems, so his rediscovery brought about their termination. Freed from the shackles of past-life wrong-doing, she found herself much more comfortable with the life at hand. Moreover, the interlife experience related at the beginning of this chapter imparted vital understanding that served to recharge Linda's energies. In the life between Rudolf and Maria, the judgement board told her, 'You will look at what went wrong and mend it.' Today in her work as an occupational therapist, she is steadily accomplishing her between-life intentions: countermanding Rudolf's murderous urges in helping daily to mend the lives of others.

11

Cry from
the Heart

'The most sublime act is to set
another before yourself.'

*William Blake,
Proverbs of Heaven*

The laboratory test results confirmed Eileen Cayley's
worst fears. Surgery was no longer a possibility; it
was a necessity. Mammograms and cell biopsies of
the large lump that had developed in her right breast
strongly indicated a cancerous tumour. In the spring
of 1974 only a surgical examination could detect the
extent of the malignancy and, according to Eileen's
doctors, the chances were high that the entire breast
would have to be removed. There was no discussion
of her chances of survival; the family's silence sought
to deny the dreadful possibilities.

The crisis left no relative or friend more distraught
than Harold Jaworski, Eileen's younger brother. Ten
days before surgery was to be performed, Harold, a
thirty-seven-year-old behavioural scientist, went to

bed early in the hope that sleep would relieve him, at least temporarily, of the lethargy that camouflaged his despair. At first all he could do was lie in the dark . . . thinking. He thought fretfully of life without Eileen, always the strong one in the family. He thought of what bereavement would mean to her husband and, especially, her two children who relied upon her for comfort, guidance and support. And the more he thought, the more anxious he became, his mind seemingly intent on replaying the same despairing theme until dawn . . .

Just when Harold believed that sleep would never come, his restlessness was suddenly dispelled and, quite spontaneously, he found himself praying to God more vehemently than ever before. He prayed that, somehow, Eileen would survive the crisis and be restored to full health. Then, plumbing the very depths of his emotions, he offered his own life in exchange for his sister's. This was more than a gesture of brotherly love: it was an impassioned cry from the heart that even Harold was at a loss to understand.

On the eve of the operation, Harold made his way to Eileen's bedside where he found his sister quietly terrified at the prospect of the next day's ordeal. He soothed her nerves as best he could before leaving the hospital to soothe his own. Miserably he made his way to an auditorium in downtown Toronto where a classical concert was being taped for the Canadian Broadcasting Corporation.

The performing chamber orchestra was well advanced in its programme of Brahms and Mozart when Harold suddenly bristled with self-awareness. There was a spotlight shining down on him! At first he looked around somewhat nervously because he felt certain the other members of the audience would be craning their necks to stare at the man singled out by this brilliant shaft of light. 'But I quickly realized,' said Harold, 'that no one was looking at me because no one else could see this light. Then a rush of ecstasy swept over me – it hit me like a tidal wave from the feet upwards. I lost all awareness of time and felt myself being drawn up into the brightness. My eyes closed and tears streamed down my cheeks. And at the heart of this most exquisite of experiences I knew . . . I *knew* that my sister would be all right.'

Harold's experience is known as cosmic consciousness – a term which springs from a book by the same name written by the Canadian Dr Richard Bucke, and first published in 1901. Writes Bucke, 'The prime characteristic of cosmic consciousness is, as its name implies, a consciousness of the cosmos, that is, of the life and order of the universe . . . Along with the consciousness of the cosmos there occurs an intellectual enlightenment or illumination which alone would place the individual on a new plane of existence – would make him almost a member of a new species. To this is added a state of moral exaltation, an indescribable feeling of elevation and joyousness, and a quickening of the moral sense, which is fully as striking and more important both to the individual and to the race than is the enhanced intellectual power. With these comes what may be called a sense of immortality, a consciousness of eternal life, not a conviction that he shall have this, but the consciousness that he has it already.' Because it incorporates brilliant illumination and loss of temporal awareness, cosmic consciousness may be a sudden, spontaneous release of early interlife memories or it may be a transient personal puncture of the membrane separating incarnate life from discarnate experience.

The next day Harold calmly returned to the hospital to await the outcome of Eileen's surgery. Once the operation was over, he approached the surgeon, who was 'shaking his head in disbelief'. Not only had the tumour been found to be benign, but it had shrunk so dramatically that it could barely be located. The non-malignant residue was cut away, the mastectomy was averted, and she went on to make a complete recovery.

One year later, Harold fell victim to hepatitis, a serious and sometimes fatal liver virus. The standard symptoms of malaise, nausea, vomiting, fatigue and jaundice engaged him in a sustained battle which kept him away from work for almost three months. For nine months thereafter, he had no reason to question his state of health. But in May 1976 he noticed that his ankles were swollen. A medical check-up subsequently detected abnormal amounts of protein in his urine and tests conducted by an internist established the need for a kidney biopsy. In August the internist determined that Harold was suffering from idiopathic membraneous glomerulonephritis, which is an obscure and clinically esoteric way of describing a potentially fatal kidney disease of unknown origin.

The internist was far from optimistic. 'It's too bad you're not a child,' he told his patient, 'because there's a greater chance of recovery with children.' When Harold learned that an adult's chances of survival were rated between ten and twenty per cent, he walked out into the sunshine feeling like a man who has just listened to his own death sentence. 'All the internist could do,' he said, 'was to tell me to cut back on my salt intake.'

Naturally Harold looked elsewhere for medical salvation. In time he found a kidney specialist at Toronto's Sunnybrook Hospital who alarmed him with the news that his hepatitis virus of the previous year was still active despite all absence of symptoms. This led to the conclusion that the covert contagion of the liver had produced what is known as an antigen-antibody complex which had gradually taken its toll on the kidneys. The severity of Harold's condition was, therefore, caused by the failure of these organs which, ailing simultaneously, had become incapable of eliminating toxins. Not that this discovery made a cure any more likely. Still, healing suggestions were always in abundance and, while one doctor ruminated out loud about the possible efficacy of a complete blood transfusion, another conjectured that the expensive and experimental drug Interferon might possibly grant immunological support.

The more Harold's condition deteriorated, the more mindful he became of his self-sacrificial pledge that appeared to have saved his sister's life. Was the Almighty proceeding inexorably towards the collection of His due? Or was Harold committed to his own demise and working unconsciously to confound the medical assistance he so desperately needed? Whatever the answer, Harold was growing steadily weaker. Hope was fast becoming a word without meaning.

For six weeks, Harold accepted doses of the drug

Cyclophosphamide. But the ineffectiveness of this treatment was revealed in creeping calcium deficiencies which softened his teeth and intermittently locked his fingers for several seconds at a time. For a while, the regular ingestion of diuretics had managed to stimulate excretion of liquids, but now his legs and ankles were swelling again. He took drugs to reduce his high cholesterol level, he was plagued with outbreaks of eczema, and he grew pale and wasted as his weight dwindled from 140 to 124 lbs. Only sporadically could Harold manage to summon up enough strength to put in an appearance at work. More and more time was spent at Sunnybrook Hospital where he was subjected interminably, or so it seemed, to blood and urine tests. 'I felt like a guinea pig in a laboratory experiment,' he said. 'The doctors didn't know how to cure me and I was going downhill fast.'

Just when the future had never looked more bleak, Harold began to be suffused by a slow, burning anger. 'It made me mad,' he said, 'to think that conventional medicine not only couldn't help me but was making things worse. I realized that the time had come for me to take responsibility for my situation.'

Harold was no stranger to parapsychology. As early as 1959, he had witnessed experiments in hypnotic regression and was well-acquainted with the theories of reincarnation and karma. Now, for the first time, he applied these theories to his predicament by asking himself, 'Is karma a factor in my illness? Can hypnotic regression to past lives succeed where orthodox methods have failed?' As he mulled over these questions, Harold renewed his reading of parapsychological material in the hospital library. One book he took down from the shelves was *Conjuring Up Philip* by Iris Owen. Flicking through its pages, he came across a chapter titled 'The Psychology of the Poltergeist Reaction' by Dr Joel L. Whitton. 'For some reason,' said Harold, 'the name stuck in my mind.' Noting that Dr Whitton called himself a medical psychologist, he asked a friend with metaphysical inclinations whether she had heard of him. The friend, who happened to be personally acquainted with Dr Whitton, explained that he was a Toronto psychiatrist and clinical hypnotist. She offered to make the necessary introductions and, just before Christmas, Harold came to recline in sickly repose on Dr Whitton's couch. Haggard, uremic and ravaged by depression, he looked as though only a miracle could save him.

Miraculous is perhaps the only fitting adjective to describe Harold's recovery over the next few weeks. He had barely begun to explore his reincarnational history under hypnosis when – within seven weeks – blood tests revealed that his liver function had returned to normal and his kidneys were quickly recuperating. By the end of March 1977 Harold felt perfectly healthy again. While the reasons for this remarkable reversal are open to speculation, it is not unreasonable to suppose that just to touch upon a previous existence in which Harold had incurred a grievous karmic debt was enough to release him from an unconscious need to surrender his own life in recompense this time around.

The precise nature of Harold's recovery is still debatable because so much remains to be learned about the physical effects of encounters with past lives. By the time his health had been restored,

Harold had yet to explore any of his previous incarnations in depth. He had made a passing acquaintance with seven lifetimes including those of a Viking raider named Thor who lived around AD 1,000; Harry, a happy-go-lucky dockworker living in Elizabethan England; Xando, a young Zoroastrian priest from seventh-century Mesopotamia; an American boy called Barrett who died in 1911 from chickenpox; and Edgar Courtney, a youthful army officer from Virginia whose death came during the early days of the American Civil War.

Seven months of hypnotic sessions had slipped by before the life of Edgar Courtney emerged as the existence which bore most heavily on the current incarnation. Session by session, Dr Whitton's investigations pieced together a tragic tale concerning Edgar and his sister Sarah, who now happens to be Harold's sister, Eileen. Their ill-fated relationship from nineteenth-century America explains most satisfactorily Harold's repressed feelings of guilt towards his sister – guilt potent enough to give rise to his ardent offer of self-sacrifice so that Eileen might live. Here's a composite account of their story compiled from Harold's trance sessions:

> Edgar and Sarah Courtney's special fondness for one another is self-evident as they grow up together on a large rural estate near Harrisonburg, Virginia. When Edgar is twelve years old and Sarah is sixteen their mutual affection extends to a brief incestuous relationship. The episode takes place when their father is away buying horses and they are picnicking in a wooded area some distance from their home. At that time, Edgar promises Sarah that he will never mention their sexual indiscretion to anyone. But several years later, when

Sarah becomes engaged to a suitor whom Edgar despises, he feels compelled to reveal their secret in order to drive the man away. The broken pact quickly becomes the gossip and scandal of the community.

In grave disgrace, Sarah is forced to leave home. Shame grants her no respite and when she can endure the loneliness and self-torment no longer she commits suicide. Edgar's remorse is bitter and unrestrained. Having enlisted in a military academy, he throws himself gratefully into the fiercest of fighting on behalf of the Confederate army when the American Civil War is declared. In one of the earliest engagements of the war, Edgar is shot in the stomach and left shoulder. He dies in agony on the battlefield, pleading to God for his life.

Slipping away from this last, horrific scene in which he clenched his stomach and felt warm, sticky blood flow over his hands, Harold was shivering when he regained consciousness. In spite of the July humidity and a room temperature of more than eighty degrees, he was obliged to rub his arms and legs for several minutes in order to generate enough body heat to make him feel comfortable. A sharp drop in body temperature occasionally results from highly emotional experiences in deep trance. Dr Whitton keeps a blanket in his office for such eventualities.

Harold's immediate past life is that of Barrett, who died at the age of seven in a community called Quincy in the United States. There are at least twelve settlements named Quincy in America, and Harold never did find out which one had been the place where he had succumbed to the ravages of chicken-pox back in 1911.

'What is the name of your home state?' Dr Whitton asked Harold.

'I don't know,' he replied in a youthful voice. 'I'll have to ask my mother.'

By earthly reckoning Harold had spent twenty-six years in the interlife between his death as Barrett and his rebirth in 1937. He didn't accompany Barrett's consciousness all the way from sickly boyhood to the between-life state. Instead, he entered the interlife shortly after transition to find his discarnate self grieving over the boy's death. Emerging, awestruck, from metaconsciousness, Harold reported:

> I was looking down at Barrett, who was lying in bed in a white nightshirt. Although I knew he was dead, I didn't want to leave him. But someone was calling me from far away and I had to go.
> I found myself in a huge room without walls and without a ceiling. I was looking up as a child might do at many other personalities who were talking among themselves. They didn't seem to have any interest in me. I was just a kid and they were busy chatting away to one another. It was strange in that I had the perspective of a child's consciousness while, in other ways, I was feeling quite old. There was no colour in the scene. It was as though I were looking at a negative or a black and white photograph.

Barrett seemed to be in the process of gradually fusing with his oversoul or eternal identity that had no time or substance or name and yet was more truly himself than any of the incarnations he had encountered during therapy. As he waited in the 'room without walls', which he perceived to be a way station for the recent survivors of physical death, he was approached by an elderly man who placed his hands on the boy's shoulders. 'That's funny,' Harold whispered in trance, 'because I don't have any shoulders. I'm not afraid any more,' he added. 'Barrett's gone . . . his body is no longer mine.'

'So, if you can't go back to Barrett, you have to go forward,' offered Dr Whitton. (Later, Harold was to remark on his irritation at this inadvertent reference to time. 'There just is no time in the place between lives,' he insisted.)

Harold then felt himself being led by the elderly man into a building like a church with a high, vaulted ceiling. His venerable escort departed, and three elderly beings dressed in white walked in and seated themselves behind a desk. The board of judgement had arrived. Harold remembers that the main thrust of their advice was that he should study during the spell between incarnations and make every effort not to waste the experience. Encouraged by Dr Whitton to search out any plans that had been laid for the forthcoming incarnation, Harold visualized his mother as she was before his birth. 'It was just as if I were looking at a photograph of her as a young woman,' he commented. Harold also saw his father and recognized him as an affectionate, supportive uncle from his life in nineteenth-century Virginia. Eileen was there too, clearly possessing the same identity as Edgar Courtney's sister, Sarah.

Harold's explorations in the between-life state confirmed that he had chosen to incarnate with the intent of rejoining his sister so that he could balance their shared karmic ledger. He learned that achievement of harmony was the primary purpose of his current life. He learned also that this purpose would be brought within reach by remembering, in his late thirties, the specific nature of the karmic involvement. Exactly how these memories would be recaptured wasn't specified, but he now understood why he had proceeded to prod himself with all manner of discomfort; he was seeking to uncover and resolve past ugliness. 'My illness didn't figure in my karmic script,' said Harold. 'I gathered it was something that I brought about in order to fulfil my plan.' This perception echoes the words of Howard Murphet, who wrote in *The Undiscovered Country*, 'Only the patterns, the outlines, of our lives are ordained and we ourselves have selected those patterns. The details we fill in as we move along the broad road of our chosen destiny.'

Today Harold is ever mindful of what he has learned from being exposed to a variety of his incarnations and the life between lives. He is infinitely more aware of his reason for being and finds as a result that he no longer has time for superficiality, frivolity and the more trivial aspects of existence. He continues to live like a man who has been raised from the dead which in actuality is not far from the truth. Once his sister had recovered so dramatically, he was convinced his offer of exchange would mean the forfeiture of his life. That was certainly the way circumstances seemed to be leading. But he was to learn there was a master plan overriding such fearful conjecture. The plan decreed that, rather than die prematurely, he must live and remember for the sake of reconciliation, for the sake of harmony.

Harold's recovery might not have taken place had he not followed his intuition and become actively involved in the healing process. Self-responsibility leads to self-determination. To accept the process of reincarnation is to accept that only by taking complete responsibility for ourselves can we hope to achieve rapid personal growth through the cycle of successive rebirths. As for Harold's sister, Eileen, she is neither aware of the inside story behind their respective medical 'miracles' nor has she been acquainted with the details of their karmic involvement. Said Harold, 'Eileen isn't comfortable with the concept of reincarnation, and I don't want to upset her.'

There's another intriguing aspect to this case study which, although unrelated to the karmic issues at stake, argues convincingly for the validity of Harold's remembered past lives. While in deep hypnosis as two of his past-life personalities – Thor the Viking and Xando the Zoroastrian priest – he began to remember and 'hear' the languages he spoke during these incarnations. When Harold was re-experiencing his life as Thor, Dr Whitton instructed him to write down, phonetically, the vocal exchanges that were taking place. Harold responded by writing twenty-two words and phrases, none of which he understood. Working independently, linguistic authorities who spoke Icelandic and Norwegian subsequently identified and translated ten of these words as being Old Norse, the language of the Vikings and the precursor of modern Icelandic. Several other words seemed to have Russian, Serbian or Slavic derivation and these were also identified. Most of the words relate to the sea – precisely the type of verbal communication that could be expected from a Viking warrior.

Dr Thor Jakobsson, a research scientist with Canada's Department of the Environment and an expert on the Icelandic language, studied the transcripts produced by Harold and concluded that many of the words – including those for 'storm', 'heart' and 'iceberg' – were 'definitely of Icelandic origin'. That some of the words had their origins in other languages only added to the authenticity of the script, said Dr Jakobsson, because the restless, warlike Vikings roamed to the far corners of Europe. 'It would be appropriate for a Viking to speak a language which contained words and phrases of other tongues of that period,' he pointed out. 'I would say this could fit the language pattern of the roving Viking.'

'Xenoglossy' is the term given to the utterance of a language unknown to the speaker while 'xenography' describes its written expression. At first Harold was somewhat bemused by his xenoglossic ability, but the genuineness of the material was impressed upon him when his urgent 'Roko! Roko!' in trance was identified with the Icelandic *rok* or 'storm'. 'We were out at sea,' said Harold, recounting the hypnotic session that produced the word in his head, 'and I could see this big storm beginning to form and I was shouting to the rowers in my boat. My mind was telling me that I was yelling "Let's get out of here!" For the experts to come up with the word "storm" made perfect sense, even though the translation was not what I had expected.'

Here are some samples of the words produced by Thor the Viking. The phonetics in bold type are those for which there is agreement in interpretation. The equivalent Icelandic word is in the second column with the English translation in the third:

YIAK	JAKI	Iceberg
LEJNESVKONJA	NES VIK	Part of land between two bays; bay
ROKO	ROK	Storm
VOLNYKIAGE		(VOLNY *in Russian means* Waves)
YIAK LEDDEREN		(JAK LED *in Serbian means* Strong ice)
HYARTA KNO-LOTTEN	HJARTA	Heart
VLOGNIA	LOGN	Calm weather
NEGI **LOKUSNO**	LOK LOKS	Container, ending, at last (NIJE USUSNO *in Serbian means* It is not tasteful)
KIAK **80 SANTI**		(80 SANTI *in Serbian means* 80 ice floes; *the 80 was written in numerals*)

Once Harold's former life as Xando was discovered, Dr Whitton hypnotized his subject as he sat at a desk holding a pencil. First, he carried him back to his birth in Mesopotamia more than 1,300 years earlier.

Then he asked him to go forward in time to the age when he was able to write and instructed him to reproduce, in the language of the day, the equivalent of such English words as 'brother', 'house', 'clothing', 'village' and so on. Holding the pencil very lightly, Harold carefully created a mysterious, Arabic-style script in a spidery, childlike hand.

'When I looked at what I had done,' said Harold, 'all I could see was a bunch of squiggles. I thought it was pure garbage.' Dr Whitton felt differently, however. Unsuccessful in matching his patient's supposed calligraphy with ancient scripts in library books, he eventually submitted the pencil markings to Dr Ibrahim Pourhadi, an expert in ancient Persian and Iranian languages at the Near Eastern Section of Washington's Library of Congress. After close examination of the samples, Dr Pourhadi maintained that the 'squiggles' were an authentic representation of the long-extinct language called *Sassanid Pahlavi*, which was used in Mesopotamia between AD 226 and 651 and bears no relation to modern Iranian.

Xenoglossy is a term coined by Dr Charles Richet (1850–1935), the French physiologist and Nobel Prize winner. The word is derived from the Greek prefix *xeno*, meaning 'strange' or 'foreign', and the word *glossa*, meaning 'tongue'. In medieval times, xenoglossy was viewed as a prime indicator of the presence of the devil. Guazzo's *Compendium Maleficorum* of 1608, a standard Catholic demonology, lists this rare and usually involuntary phenomenon as one of forty-seven probable signs of demonic possession.

Over the past one hundred years, xenoglossy has

been generally considered to suggest the outpouring of subconscious memory. Cases have been examined by eminent parapsychological researchers ranging from William James to Dr Ian Stevenson. The growing incidence of past-life therapy since the early 1970s has produced numerous examples of trance subjects holding forth in foreign tongues to which they have not been exposed in the current life. The range of such hypnotic diction is vast and includes modern European languages, ancient Chinese, and even jungle dialects. However, Harold is quite possibly the only human being to demonstrate the ability to communicate in two verifiable languages that no longer exist.

12

When Remorse Bleeds

'Who, doomed to go in company with Pain,
And Fear, and Bloodshed, miserable train!
Turns his necessity
to glorious gain . . .'

William Wordsworth,
Character of the Happy Warrior

Thursday, April 10, 1980, should have been another
routine day for social worker Jenny Saunders. Aiming
to be at her desk by nine, she got up shortly before
seven-thirty, flung on a housecoat, and padded out
of the bedroom in search of a cup of coffee. She didn't
get very far. Her bare feet were just about to cross
the living room carpet when they paused in mid-
stride; her still-sleepy eyes widened in amazement.

Jenny's attention was drawn to the nearest wall
where, at about head height, four or five blotches of
a deep red substance were splattered directly above
the baby's room of the doll's house she had treasured

since childhood. She craned forward for a closer inspection. The blotches looked *exactly* like blood. Quickly, she scanned her hands and body for tell-tale cuts. No, she wasn't bleeding. Her next thought was that she had somehow spilled some tomato ketchup the night before. But this idea, too, was dismissed because she remembered she hadn't been near the ketchup bottle. Besides, the stains looked more like blood than ketchup. It was all very disconcerting. When Jenny finally made her cup of coffee, she was hardly aware of what she was doing. Sipping absentmindedly, she puzzled in vain.

The day at work was a busy one. There were always heavy demands on Jenny's time and expertise as she researched case studies for an agency dedicated to the welfare of mentally retarded children. For as long as she could remember, Jenny, twenty-eight, had wanted to work with the mentally handicapped. She didn't mind the long hours and modest salary because she was in love with her job, applying her considerable energies with a selflessness her colleagues found almost daunting. On this particular day, as on many others, the case studies kept Jenny at her desk until well past seven o'clock in the evening. So it was hardly surprising that, long before returning home, she had quite forgotten about the marks on her wall. Only after she turned the key in the front door of her apartment, flicked on the light, and entered the living-room was she forcibly reminded of what had been left behind.

Jenny quailed at the sight of fresh 'blood' on the wall over the doll's house. New splashes had appeared close to where the marks seen that morning had dried in ragged drips. She hesitated momentarily before walking over to examine the coagulation, stretching out an inquiring finger to encounter the consistency, as well as the appearance, of blood. The stains were somehow materializing on the surface of the white-painted wall; they weren't seeping through from the other side.

Over the next few days more spots and splatters appeared. On separate occasions three of Jenny's close friends verified the bizarre phenomenon. These friends entered the apartment, witnessed the marks, left with Jenny for an hour or more, and returned to find that fresh stains had appeared during their absence. Said one witness, Michelle Ouellette, 'I thought that, maybe, Jenny was somehow creating this stuff while sleepwalking. But that explanation was rejected when we got back to her apartment to find new markings that simply weren't there before we left to see a movie. I could hardly believe my eyes!'

Although this extraordinary situation left Jenny feeling more apprehensive than alarmed, she could no longer work without a nagging preoccupation with the gory goings-on at home. Curiously, she had no desire to wipe away the marks which dominated her thoughts. They covered more and more of the wall and even spread to the side of the television set. Not that she was enjoying this expanding abstract mural. She continually fretted over why this was happening and what she could do about it. But indecision claimed her until she awoke one morning to find that a bloody trickle had appeared on the peaked roof of the doll's house. That was the day Jenny telephoned her parents for advice.

For Jenny to call her parents at all indicated a

certain desperation. She rarely saw her mother and father. Family get-togethers were usually limited to the Christmas season, weddings and funerals. Nevertheless, Mr and Mrs Saunders responded readily to their daughter's phone call and arrived at the apartment that very evening. Their examination of the stains, conducted with muttered consternation, led to an abrupt appraisal. 'This place is haunted,' Jenny's mother declared.

Haunting might have seemed the obvious suggestion to anyone who acknowledges metaphysical reality, this possibility having already occurred to Jenny's friends as well as to Jenny herself. But no one had thus far voiced this interpretation quite so strenuously. Her mother's insistence on 'possession by an evil spirit of some kind' left Jenny so flustered that she fled her apartment in terror. That night, a Friday, she spent sleeplessly at the home of a friend. The next day she found herself another apartment in downtown Toronto and on Sunday moved in with all her belongings, including the doll's house. Meanwhile, Jenny's father managed to track down Dr Whitton, who was tucked away in a vacation hideaway near Peterborough, Ontario. Having seen Dr Whitton interviewed on television as an expert on 'spooky' phenomena, be begged him to help his daughter.

Dr Whitton agreed to see Jenny on his return. He had just one question for Mr Saunders: 'Do you have a sample of the bloodstains?' Too late, Jenny was thinking along similar lines. Once her fears had subsided, she returned to the apartment to take photographs and scrape the walls for evidence but, on arrival, found that the superintendent of the apartment building had spent the previous day repainting the vacated living-room. Attempting to remove the stains with a scrubbing brush dipped in a bucket of soapy water, he had discovered the markings had permeated the plaster beneath the paintwork. His response was to apply a coat of dark grey latex, ensuring that the 'blood on the wall' was lost forever.

By the time Jenny showed up at Dr Whitton's office for her first consultation she was convinced she had attracted a wicked ghost with demonstrably lurid powers. Dr Whitton, however, thought otherwise. Having investigated several cases of poltergeist and psychokinetic activity (a poltergeist is the work of a mischievous spirit, while psychokinesis is the movement and/or materialization of objects by the mind of a living person) he felt that Jenny's psychological state must have produced the mysterious bloodstains *as a symbolic expression of internal conflict.* According to psychoanalyst Nandor Fodor, unwitting behaviour of this kind is indicative of 'a bundle of projected repressions'.

Those rare individuals who can trigger PK, as psychokinesis is commonly known, never act just once; they have a history of such manifestations. Two major questions, therefore, demanded answers: Did Jenny have a history of psychokinetic activity? And, if so, what events had provoked the deep conflict that was producing blood on a wall?

The response to the first question was overwhelmingly in the affirmative. Jenny disclosed that she had been connected with, and presumably was responsible for, an array of psychokinetic happenings. Dr Whitton, who came to call Jenny 'the PK lady', would later witness her unconscious powers in the form of flashing lights in his office during a counselling session. For now, he was made aware of the following strange occurrences:

- Tumblers waiting to dry in Jenny's dish rack had exploded spontaneously.

- Curtains closed across the front window of a friend's apartment had parted noisily, and to their full extent, while Jenny and a friend chatted away.

- Visiting her parents' house for dinner, Jenny sat staring at an empty bamboo bird cage that was hanging from the ceiling by a heavy chain. Inside the cage was perched an artificial bird made of colourful synthetic material. Just as Jenny was wondering whether a real bird had ever lived there, the cage and its four-foot-long chain came crashing down. After hitting the floor, the chain disappeared or dematerialized, and has never been found.

- A friend had given Jenny a bud vase made of lead crystal. This friend later telephoned with an invitation to visit her apartment. But Jenny didn't want to go and, feeling uncomfortable, started to make excuses. As she replaced the receiver, the PK lady struck again. Jenny looked on in bewilderment as the bud vase, which was standing on a dresser across the room, broke off at the stem, fell to the floor and smashed to pieces.

- Reluctantly Jenny had allowed a male acquaintance to return to her apartment after a dinner engagement. He had insisted on coming back 'for a coffee', and it wasn't long before he started making sexual advances. These Jenny neither wanted nor encouraged, and the thought flashed into her mind: 'If only the time was much later, he would feel obliged to leave.' As that thought took shape, all four clocks in the apartment, including Jenny's wristwatch, jumped ahead to show a time of 1.37 A.M. Her visitor promptly got up and left. Closing the door behind him, Jenny turned on the radio to establish the correct time. The 9.00 news was drawing to a close.

The question of inner conflict was much more difficult to answer. Assertive and purposeful in her professional dealings, Jenny was exceedingly shy and easily intimidated in a situation of social intimacy. Although she had never been treated by a psychiatrist or even her family doctor for any sort of emotional problem, her demeanour suggested that she was paralysed with anxiety. It was clear to Dr Whitton that if she was indeed torn by inner conflict, that conflict was deeply repressed. Several hour-long sessions were needed to elicit the most basic information about her life. Apparently unable to relate specific details, she talked discursively about a miserable childhood. As a teenager, she had felt so depressed and misunderstood that she had worked at three jobs just to get herself out of the house. But conflict? 'No, not really,' said Jenny. Dr Whitton was aware that such a reaction was typical of those who are raised in severely brutalizing environments; they are emotionally repressed and complain rarely, if at all, about their treatment. In his book *The Borderline Syndromes*, Michael H. Stone, MD, describes a 'subtle form of thought disorder' in patients who have been violently abused during childhood. He writes: 'Feelings are not remembered, or cannot be labelled properly, or are extinguished before they reach a state of conscious awareness.'

So why did the PK lady deliberately, if unconsciously, make blood flow on her living-room wall on April 10? Dr Whitton had observed many patients who, following the unconscious dictates of decisions made during the interlife, have precipitated drastic or spectacular events which led them to search out the origin of their difficulties. Perhaps the blood-splashed wall was an example of what has been dubbed 'anniversary phenomena'. That is to say, the PK manifestation could have been produced on a date redolent with traumatic significance for the patient. Unaware of any personal anniversary of emotional import, Jenny couldn't confirm this hypothesis. Instead, she whispered with all the reticence of confession: 'I got pregnant last summer. I went for an abortion – nobody knew about it.'

Dr Whitton applied himself to this revelation with all the zeal of a detective hounding a solitary but very promising lead. He appreciated at once that Jenny's abortion had left her severely oppressed by guilt. Further, he discovered that even though she cared passionately for mentally retarded children and taught parenting skills to handicapped adults, Jenny was terrified of having a baby. He noted that her lost child was conceived on June 23, 1979 – an easily retrievable date because that was the only time Jenny had engaged in sexual intercourse over many years. Dr Whitton calculated that this should have meant, all being well, a delivery in early April. The records of Jenny's attending gynaecologist at Toronto General Hospital provided, explicitly, the confirmation he was seeking. If the baby had survived, its birth would have been expected on April 10, 1980 – the very day that blood had first appeared on Jenny's wall.

At this point, Jenny revealed another PK incident with obvious links to her pregnancy. The previous year, in her apartment laden with greenery, she had been tending a plant called *Helxine soleirolii*, better known as 'baby's-tears'. For no apparent reason, this delicate but vibrantly healthy plant shrivelled and died sometime during the early hours of September 2, shortly before she was admitted to hospital for the abortion. In hospital, an examination revealed that an abortion was no longer necessary as the foetus she was carrying had died three days earlier. That's when Jenny remembered the 'baby's-tears' – the plant had dramatically withered and turned brown at the same time her embryonic child had ceased to be. This spontaneous abortion – known, clinically, as a 'missed abortion' – was not unusual, such miscarriages occurring in at least ten to twenty per cent of all pregnancies. Psychologically, however, the psychokinetic activity linked with Jenny's womb indicated extraordinary emotional intensity as well as supercharged psychic ability.

Psychokinesis (from *psyche*, mind; *kinesis*, motion) was once thought to indicate demonic possession but is now known to be the physical manifestation, psychically induced, of subliminal tension. While some people are able to perform PK feats at will, others act unconsciously. During the late 1960s and early 1970s, teenager Matthew Manning – whose rare abilities were tested by Dr Whitton and Dr A. R. George Owen in Toronto in 1974 – unconsciously produced sensational examples of PK phenomena. At Matthew's home in Cambridge, England, light ornaments, chairs, cutlery, ashtrays, baskets, plates, a small coffee table, and a score of other articles were moved mysteriously from one part of the house to another. As the number of incidents escalated, erratic taps and creaks sounded throughout the day and night in all parts of the house. After the Manning family moved to the village of Linton in 1968, heavy tables were occasionally placed one on top of the other, and beds were frequently stripped or even overturned. In Matthew's dormitory at Oakham School, Cambridgeshire, heavy steel bunk beds moved of their own accord and, on one occasion, fourteen table knives were 'thrown' against walls and beds. For a while, sleeping in the dormitory was made virtually impossible by the mysterious appearance of broken glass, nails, plates, pebbles and other odds and ends.

During the 1970s, a boyish-looking Israeli named Uri Geller amazed the Western world with his feats of metal bending. Displaying conscious PK ability, he left television studios and scientific laboratories strewn with twisted spoons, forks and keys. Geller subjected himself to all kinds of testing, yet neither scientists nor experts from the Society for American Magicians could logically explain his powers. History is replete with instances of psychokinesis, including manifestations similar to those invoked by Jenny Saunders. In 1919, in the presence of newspaper reporters and other witnesses, oil and water ran from the walls and ceilings of the Rectory at Swanton Novers, Suffolk.

Dr Whitton's preliminary investigation confirmed his original opinion that psychokinetic activity was Jenny's way of ventilating tension as well as indicating deeply repressed trauma. He wasn't surprised that Jenny had made no conscious connection between her PK energies and the appearance of the bloodstains or that she hadn't tried to wipe away the markings from her wall. He knew that Jenny wanted both to remember and to forget at the same time. While she had tried valiantly to repress all memory of her aborted child, another part of her mind was equally determined to prevent amnesia, the blood-stains being a form of release that probably kept her sane. But they also represented a seething, deep-seated disturbance that demanded inspection.

Faced with the task of exposing the heart of Jenny's troubles, Dr Whitton began by taking her back to childhood by means of hypnosis. In sessions that stretched over the next two years, every important event up to the age of eleven was steadily exhumed and paraded before her conscious mind. The mask of the timid, expressionless young woman was stripped away by the trance state as Jenny gagged and grim-aced in pain and anger. How horrible it was to relive every foul experience that she had consigned to the vaults of oblivion. And yet, paradoxically, how re-leasing! Together, doctor and patient discovered that Jenny, from a very early age, had been the victim of relentless brutality and sexual torture. Just to sur-vive, she had repressed all conscious memory of the horror that was childhood.

As an adult, Jenny felt nothing but fear and hatred for her mother; no amount of repression could ob-scure her emotional orientation. Even so, she was profoundly shocked to discover that this woman had been, not merely uncaring and neglectful, but the veritable scourge of her formative years. In trance, Jenny learned that, starting at the age of five, she had been raped by her mother on innumerable occasions with sticks and broom handles. She realized that two scars close to her genitals, scars whose origin she had always questioned, stemmed from her mother's wild lunges with a pair of scissors. Horrifyingly, Jenny witnessed her mother's avowed intent. 'I want to make you so that no man will ever want you,' she had told the little girl.

At first, Jenny couldn't believe that her own mother had committed such atrocities. Several sessions were required before the reality of her memories pervaded her consciousness. Swimming hypnotically through the torment of her once-obliterated past, she re-experienced her mother's beatings, sexual depravity, screaming fits, and her own lengthy periods of solitary confinement. Jenny's father, the public relations director of a large electronics company, probably never even guessed at his daughter's distress. He was always working, always away from home.

Jenny's earliest captured memory is of lying hungrily in her crib. A door opened on the far side of the room, and a baby's milk bottle was thrown down beside her. Not yet able to hold the bottle with her tiny hands, little Jenny squirmed with great difficulty into a position which enabled her to close her mouth around the rubber teat. Such maternal insufficiency, to put it mildly, presaged the infliction to come.

Jenny's mother, a habitual drug taker who has been confined periodically to psychiatric institutions, indirectly accused her daughter, as she grew older, of being a murderer. She kept reiterating that Jenny was born shortly after a stillbirth. 'This baby had to die so that you might live,' she would say. Contact with other members of the family later established that this stillborn child was nothing but the product of the mother's disturbed imagination. But as far as

Jenny was concerned these primal feelings of guilt were as real as the blows to her body. The guilt lingered in her subconscious mind, lying dormant until being violently reactivated by the intended abortion in 1979. Once again, she was 'killing' a foetus so that she might live.

The hypnotic sessions were not always successful in drawing memories all the way to the surface. Sometimes, Jenny's dreams completed the process. At other times, the unseen hand of psychokinesis provided the necessary incentive for conscious recall. One morning, Jenny awoke to find that a corner of the hardwood floor in her apartment had been streaked more than twenty times with a red, greasy substance. As much as she was at a loss to explain this – she neither wore red lipstick nor had any red crayons in the apartment – such events no longer surprised her. But she did let out an involuntary gasp on climbing into the shower – daubed on her right thigh was a broad black mark about five inches long. In the next session, Jenny recovered a memory in which, at six years of age, she was rummaging among her mother's bottles of nail polish. She selected a shade of red, which was to match the red streaks on the hardwood floor, and proceeded to paint a section of her parents' bedroom wall. When her mother discovered the artist at work, she beat her with a belt. Jenny's legs were bruised so badly that she was unable to attend school for an entire week.

On another occasion, Jenny awoke to find blood-like smudges on the bottle of tranquillizers Dr Whitton had prescribed to help her sleep through the sessions' often disturbing aftermath. The blood-stained bottle turned out to be the catalyst for recalling memories of her mother's massive ingestion of various pills. These instances of psychokinesis, incidentally, granted Dr Whitton the opportunity to witness and photograph the phenomena.

The excavation of Jenny's memories eased many of her anxieties, made her less fearful of people, removed the fear of her mother (though the hatred remained), and left her feeling much more positive about herself. So positive, in fact, that she applied for, and gained, a more responsible position with another agency serving the mentally handicapped. At about this time, in August 1981, Dr Whitton summarized the case of Jenny Saunders before the Tenth International Parascience Conference at the University of Toronto. But even as he presented his professional colleagues with detailed descriptions of psychokinetic phantasmagoria, Dr Whitton was only too aware of the incompleteness of the case of Jenny Saunders. Jenny was still far from free of her problems. Her guilt feelings had diminished, but they were by no means eradicated. She was still terrified at the prospect of being a mother. She had a phobia of sharp knives. And she suffered from an irrational aversion to her father, a phobia which could not be substantiated by regained childhood memories.

She was also distressed by a symptom she described as a 'crotch-knot'. This left her, when sexually stimulated, sensing pain rather than pleasure — pain that would mutate into murderous rage. As a result, Jenny had led a sexually reclusive life for years. She was not quite celibate but she was loath to arouse latent feelings of anger that would make her want to kill whoever was touching her. If the anger persisted, she would turn it against herself by indulging in fantasies of cutting out her clitoris with a pair of scissors. In the light of her mother's brutality, Dr Whitton found this reaction perfectly understandable. But, having exhausted her childhood memories without alleviating this symptom, he supposed that its source – as well as the source of other recalcitrant symptoms – might lie deeper than the current incarnation. The time had come for Jenny to be carried back beyond infancy. Seeking the origin of her fear of motherhood, Dr Whitton regressed her to a life in seventeenth-century England. She managed the transition effortlessly . . .

The year is 1689, and London is a pitiless place to be for a single woman with a mentally retarded child. Everyone prevails upon Lucy Bowden to get rid of her three-year-old daughter because she is handicapped. 'It's a burden,' people tell her, 'nothing but a burden.' Most people think the retarded child should be either put to death or abandoned on the edge of town. But Lucy, twenty-one, loves and treasures her little girl more than anything in the world. Largely supported by money from Lucy's family, they live together in a third-floor attic in Whitechapel. Lucy keeps the child hidden away, fearful that someone might, however well-meaningly, kidnap the girl and turn her loose. Always ensuring the child is locked in when leaving home, Lucy never stays away for very long. Well, almost never . . .

One day, after shopping for provisions at the local market, Lucy calls at an alehouse to join a gathering of friends. They buy her ale and, not being a drinker, Lucy becomes light-headed and stays longer, much longer, than intended. Several hours pass before she realizes with alarm how much time has elapsed. Scooping up her groceries, she rushes back to the attic. As she turns

*the corner into her street she sees black smoke billowing
from a house – her house. Beneath the pall, the building
is furiously ablaze. Lucy pushes her way through a
crowd of onlookers only to realize there's no hope of
rescuing her little girl. No hope at all. Overpowered by
despair, she chides herself ceaselessly: If only she had
left for home earlier. If only . . .*

Returning to normal consciousness, Jenny gasped
with relief just to know she was no longer in Lucy's
body. She was beginning to appreciate why she was
so afraid of motherhood. She was making sense, too,
of the underlying motivation that drove her to work
diligently and selflessly on behalf of mentally handicapped children. The next session carried Jenny
further in this English life . . .

*Lucy is strapped to a horizontal wooden wheel which
is being slowly rotated by two priests in the dank and
musty confines of a church cellar. She is dressed in a
white smock. The priests, clenching handles attached
to the side of the wheel, wander in and out of her
swaying vision. There is chanting, prayer, incantation.
Lucy has surrendered willingly to this ordeal in order
to make the devil dizzy and thereby drive his possessing
evil from her body. Yes, Lucy tells herself, surely the
men of God are right. Surely it was the devil who made
her stay so long in the alehouse, long enough for her
child to perish, abandoned, in the fire.*

*Stricken with grief and remorse, Lucy had visited her
Anglican priest. He had listened to her tragic tale,
proffered his condolences and told her that her extended
absence from the attic was so out of character that it
must have been the devil's work. And so he brought
her to this place of exorcism.*

The walls revolve. Vertigo . . . nausea . . . forgiveness

*. . . redemption . . . nausea. Towards the end of the
ceremony, a pitcher of lamb's blood, symbolizing the
blood of Christ, is poured down a wall.*

Another bloodstained wall. Once again, distant
echoes were investing the present with a certain
clarity. Therapeutically, however, there was still
much work to be done involving yet another wall of
blood. Dr Whitton guided Jenny into her immediate
past life . . .

*Angela is five years old when her parents abandon
her on the steps of a Chicago orphanage in 1846. At the
age of sixteen, she steals some money and runs away
from the harshness of the institution. Living by her
wits, she travels deep into the Midwest, winding up in
a frontier town called Colona in Colorado Territory.*

*Being a pretty girl, Angela is readily hired as a bar-
maid in a local saloon, where she soon avails herself of
extra money by working part-time as a prostitute. Her
allure does not go unnoticed by the town physician, a
married man who becomes so captivated that he pays
the saloon keeper a hefty retainer in order to have her
all to himself. In time, Angela falls in love with this
man. She becomes pregnant, wants desperately to have
the child, and the doctor delivers a healthy baby boy
in a room above the bar.*

*Despite the sordid backdrop to their relationship,
Angela is deeply in love with the doctor and feels happy
about the way her life has progressed. But her content-
ment cannot withstand interference from the local parson, a preacher of fundamentalist persuasion who
becomes incensed that a 'scarlet woman' has given
birth to the doctor's child. Vowing to have the baby
placed in an institution where its moral sanctity can be*

preserved, he blackmails the physician into supporting this plan.

As Angela is convalescing in bed with her newborn baby, the parson strides into the room with the doctor and two town officials. Noting the crestfallen look on the doctor's face, she senses the purpose of the visit and quickly becomes hysterical. When Angela fails to prevent one of the officials from seizing her baby, she flings herself to one side to reach for a shotgun she keeps under the bed. The other official lunges forward at the sight of the gun and, as he grapples with her, the weapon discharges, killing both the infant and the man who cradles him in his arms. The close-range blast splatters man and baby across the wall behind them.

Mute, devastated, Angela slumps to the floor in a state of shock. The doctor flees the room and the parson is about to walk downstairs to the bar when he is met by six drunken cowboys excited by the sound of gunfire. The parson wastes no time in delivering a prejudicial account of Angela's actions and incites the men to mete out punishment appropriate to a murderous whore.

The cowboys drag Angela from her room and carry her to a nearby warehouse where cattle are routinely slaughtered. To the sound of jeers and raucous laughter, she is stripped of her nightgown and gang-raped. Then she is strung up from a broad wooden beam and bull-whipped until the flesh hangs in fronds from her body. When she is close to death, Angela is cut down and skinned with hunting knives.

The horrendous suffering of Angela's final hours left Jenny racking with convulsions which gradually receded as the death experience took over. Reassured that she would remain in trance, she left her flayed body lying in a pool of blood to enter metaconsciousness: her first, cautious entry into the life between lives. Hovering over the heads of her assailants, she watched her corpse being picked up and trailed through the warehouse to be dumped, finally, on a heap of rotting animal carcasses. Having departed from her body, Angela ceased to suffer physically. But there was no reprieve from the psychological pain. This was the pain of guilt, the remorse of having reached for the shotgun, the anguish of having killed her own child.

In re-experiencing Angela's guilt, Jenny wept noisily for the first and only time in front of Dr Whitton. When upset as a child, she had learned not to make a sound as any form of complaint invited more brutal treatment from her mother. So deeply inculcated was this pattern of behaviour that, even under hypnosis, Jenny neither cried nor groaned nor even whimpered . . . until being faced with the pain of Angela's tragedy.

In the weeks that followed, Jenny came to feel brighter about her life. Her phobia of sharp knives, which originated with her skinning by the cowboys, became a thing of the past. The painful 'crotch-knot', which had its source in the gang rape, shrank into insignificance. And Jenny's mystifying fear of her father was explained and banished simultaneously with the realization that he was one of the ruffians who had raped and skinned her on that day of infamy in nineteenth-century Colorado. Today Jenny still finds difficulty in loving and trusting her father. But she is, at least, able to cope with this problem intellectually. After re-experiencing her incarnation as Angela, she was able to give him a hug for the first time.

As a result of the greater self-understanding gained

through past-life therapy, Jenny's psychokinetic talents have failed to recur unbidden. In search of the origins of this remarkable ability, Dr Whitton carried her once more into trance. There she encountered Elee, a white-robed priestess in a mystical order based in Rome during the second century AD. Elee spoke of being able to move and alter objects with her mind. She said the powers were used ritualistically and that she was responsible for training girls to exercise similar abilities. Following this trance revelation, Jenny has attempted, with some success, to resurrect these long-lost abilities. No longer at the mercy of her neglected powers, the PK lady is striving to draw this psychic heritage into conscious awareness.

In three years, Jenny had learned a lot about herself. Escorted to her mind's observation deck, she had peered into the very entrails of her trauma. Her reward was freedom from self – the self she had once been but with whom she no longer needed or wanted to be associated. From personal experience, she had come to recognize that there are no such things as accidents and inexplicable happenings, finding that everything in her extended past had its meaning, purpose and reason to be. Indeed, while the appearance of bloodstains on Jenny's wall appeared to be the most unfathomable of mysteries back in April 1980, this complex case study shows that answers can be found providing the search is pressed to its furthest conclusion.

Yet, it seems, there are always more questions. The very intricacy of Jenny's case begged for an explanation of the overriding intent of the progression from Lucy to Angela to Jenny. Dr Whitton knew that metaconsciousness was equal to this challenge, and he guided his patient yet again into the life between the lives of Angela and Jenny.

'What do you see?' he asked gently.

Jenny appeared to be sensing and feeling such intensity that he desisted from interrupting her timeless, spaceless glide in the *bardo*. Eventually he posed the question again, slightly differently . . .

'*Who* do you see?'

> *Myself . . . chains . . . I'm wearing a black robe . . . There are chains on my wrists and ankles . . . The Judgement . . . I feel so much shame. So much guilt and shame. I don't want to . . .*

Haltingly Jenny described how three sincere, contented beings were waiting to offer comfort and reassurance. She felt overawed by their wisdom and compassion and, believing herself unworthy of their attentions, was reluctant to approach them. All she could do was blame herself for making mistakes in her life as Angela, reserving her strongest recriminations for the impetuous action which killed her child. But the Three maintained their supportive presence, and Jenny felt the chains slip from her wrists and ankles as she came to understand that the situation wasn't quite so hopeless. The judgement board assisted her in evaluating the life just completed and entered into a discussion of various crucial episodes.

Jenny's trust in the three beings strengthened as the review of her life unfolded. Then, as if to stimulate greater comprehension of her eternal purpose, she was granted the realization that Lucy's child and

Angela's child were elements of the same soul which, for its own karmic reasons, *needed* two short lives. (Incarnate existence may be cut short specifically to fulfil a requirement of interlife planning. From the perspective of metaconsciousness, physical death – no matter when it occurs – always promotes learning and growth.)

Jenny next saw herself standing in a long dress among a group of children. Only one child noticed her presence – a child she recognized at once as the same being that Lucy and Angela had mothered. The infant toddled over to her and tugged at her dress, as if wanting to be picked up and held. Jenny responded with a warm inner glow and felt her abdomen swelling. She had the distinct impression that later in the current life this child could once again be hers.

Jenny was eager to gain all the knowledge she could from her prolonged immersion in the interlife. Angela, she learned, hadn't even begun to come to terms with karmic issues and, in order to make any progress as Jenny, she first needed to bring herself to the point where Angela had left off. In other words she needed Angela's trauma, or its equivalent, and – on the advice of the Three – she grimly decided to undergo the horrific childhood described earlier in this chapter. Jenny's discarnate identity, glimpsing the extraordinary challenges of the forthcoming incarnation, tried to resist the pull to the Earth plane. 'I'm not ready to go back – I'm afraid,' she told a luminous figure she identified as her guide who appeared to preside over the process of rebirth.

Reluctantly accepting the recommendations of the judgement board, Jenny made the decision to work at discharging karma in the life to come by implementing the full force of her personality to strive for the welfare of mentally handicapped children. Furthermore she understood that her aborted pregnancy had been specifically selected to initiate comprehension of her troubled past. It was, after all, the pregnancy, allied with the psychokinetic phenomena, that brought Jenny into therapy. 'You must face the fear and the anger head-on,' she was told by the Three. This is exactly what she did.

Karmically speaking, it would appear that Jenny had by no means earned the horrendous childhood she was to endure. After all, had she not striven to preserve her retarded child in England? Had she not done her utmost to save the infant born in Colorado? Undoubtedly the answer is yes, but Jenny's view of her behaviour in both these situations was distorted by her guilt-ridden perception. And, to a large extent, one's perception is one's reality, both here and in the hereafter. As Lucy, she came to believe that, by lingering absentmindedly at the alehouse for a few hours, she had unconsciously invited her baby's death in accordance with the wishes of others. As Angela she was incapable of forgiving herself for the act of murder, no matter how inadvertently it had occurred. Later she appeared in chains before the judgement board because she chose to do so. Although the chains slipped from her wrists at the encouragement of the Three, she was in opposition to the idea that she relieve herself of blame. Still trapped in the mesh of her own seeming wrongdoing, she was constrained to bring more trouble on her own head in the current life. Trouble, lots of it, is what she felt she deserved. Until reliving the life between lives, Jenny was unable to accept that she was anything but guilty, guilty, guilty.

In the interlife, Jenny scanned her karmic script and saw that it was drawn up in great detail until her early thirties. By that time, if all went according to plan, she would have overcome negative karmic influences. Only then could she decide what to do with the rest of her life.

As this book goes to press, Jenny Saunders is thirty-four years old and contemplating a career change. While recognizing the past importance of her work with the mentally handicapped, she is no longer driven to pursue this line of service. Having shaken off her dread of motherhood, she is determined to have a child of her own. For the first time in her life, she is actively looking for someone with whom to share this experience. Just in case a suitable partner can't be found before her biological clock runs down, she has successfully applied to become a mother by means of artificial insemination. Her application was supported by a glowing recommendation from Dr Whitton. 'After all she's been through,' he stated, 'a more loving and dedicated mother than Jenny Saunders will be hard to find.'

13

A Guide to Self-exploration
of the Interlife

'To open the individual path inward
is the most exalted of human
endeavours . . .'

James S. Perkins,
Through Death to Rebirth

*The infinite can only be apprehended by a faculty
superior to reason, by entering into a state from
which the finite self must withdraw.*

When Plotinus, the Greek philosopher, wrote these
lines in the third century, he was describing, know-
ingly or not, the primary principle in personal exploration of the between-life state. In order to 'explore
the River of Soul; whence or in what order you have
come', as the prophet Zoroaster advocated, the everyday world must be left far behind. Then, and only then
– through relaxation, concentration, diligence and the
patience to wait for results – is it possible to seek out
and fasten on knowledge of the life between life.

Regression by a hypnotist may be a faster method of uncovering memories from between incarnations, but anyone who is willing to persist in perfecting a method of visualization has every chance of success. Moreover, once self-exploration is mastered, it can be practised at will, without having to rely upon the mediation of another person.

Visualization is no more than a means to an end, a way of programming the subconscious to reveal experiences of the *bardo* or past lives, whichever the seeker desires. Of the wide variety of techniques available, Dr Whitton favours a traditional method known as the 'celestial sanctum' that has proven itself across the centuries. This step-by-step introduction to inner attunement is thought to have originated with the Knights Templars, a Christian mystical order which flourished at the time of the crusades.

The basic idea is simple. Envision a huge and magnificent cathedral – depending on religious preference, this may be a temple, mosque or synagogue – floating far above the Earth. This soaring structure, the celestial sanctum, incorporates a vast library containing the Akashic Records. As we mentioned, the Akashic Records bear the indelible imprint on the ether of all that has happened – a full and intricate accounting of the lives and interlives of every soul that has ever existed. In bringing the sanctum into conscious thought, consider that no library could ever hold the vast quantity of information stored in this celestial collection.

Practising the visualization exercise that follows demands both reverence and faith: reverence for the immortal intelligence behind the knowledge and faith that the knowledge will be revealed. Gautama Buddha once said, 'If the mind be fixed on the acquirement of any object, that object will be attained.'

As a preliminary exercise in memory stimulation, imagine that you are looking at a photograph album of your childhood. Turn to the page that holds a picture of your tenth birthday. Look at yourself and those who surround you. You will not only recognize, naturally enough, the faces in the photograph, but you will also be aware of events and emotions outside the picture frame. You might say to yourself, for example, 'That was the year I was friends with Sally. The next year she went to another school' or 'My brother Jimmy still had his arm in a cast after falling from the tree house.' The picture triggers other memories that extend beyond the limits of the frame. So it will be when you enter the etheric library and take down the book containing whatever past life you choose to examine.

Since interlife memories are unlikely to be remembered sequentially, they can be as confusing as a hologram which, at first glance, reveals no more than a meaningless jumble of rippling lines. Under the glare of laser light, the hologram will be transformed into a three-dimensional picture just as the interlife will produce meaningful imagery as soon as the percipient exercises his or her thought processes. To meddle with Descartes, 'I think, therefore I see.' The photograph and the hologram analogies are mentioned simply as an aid to entice memories from hiding. Some people may find their memories are revealed in the form of a film. If this is the case, imagine taking a videotape cassette – rather than a book or photo album – from the library shelf, carrying it into a projection room and inserting it into a cassette player to start recall flowing at the climax of the visualization exercise.

Here it must be stressed that the exercise is aimed only at recovering knowledge of events *that have taken place*. This data already exists and cannot be changed. When information comes to mind there's only one way to tell whether a vein of genuine memory has been struck – deep, inner certainty will accompany the imagery. If, on the other hand, the scenes or flashes of scenes appear to be nothing but fantasy and imagination, they most probably are. The golden rule declares: If you doubt what you see, don't believe it.

Those who have difficulty visualizing will benefit from training themselves to see, in their mind's eye, a flickering candle or a specific geometric image such as a square or a circle. It is also helpful to step into a room, survey its contents as carefully as possible, and then close your eyes in an effort to reconstruct all that you have seen. Anyone who doubts their ability to visualize clearly should repeat these preliminary exercises several times before the first attempt is made to enter the celestial sanctum. If the most determined efforts at visualization are unsuccessful, the information should still be attainable: it will be perceived intuitively rather than seen, either at the time of the visualization or at some later point.

We are now almost ready for the measured induction which you may choose to read yourself or have read to you by a partner. You can also tape yourself reading aloud, then play it back when you are ready to begin the self-exploration. Before you start, however, still further preparation of mind may be useful. It cannot be stressed too strongly that self-exploration of one's past cannot be taken lightly; a voyeuristic approach is to be sternly resisted. To venture into the interlife is to explore the meaning and purpose of one's being, and such an important quest necessitates reverence and humility. The celestial sanctum 'must represent to each person the highest degree of purity and sanctity of which he is capable', according to Charles Dana Dean, who wrote a pamphlet about the sanctum's origins and purposes. Now, to the final preparatory ritual . . .

First, find a quiet place where the exercise may proceed undisturbed. Wash your hands in clean water and dry them well. This symbolizes the cleansing of the body. Next, spend several minutes in utter relaxation – lying down, perhaps, or sitting in a favourite chair – to relieve yourself progressively of all workaday thoughts and negativity. To assist in this process, you can purge your aura of negative influences by simply closing your eyes, concentrating on positive thoughts, and running your hands swiftly over the outline of the body, as close to the skin as possible without touching. Expect to feel a tingling sensation as this takes place. Imagine that you are sweeping away everything cloying or distracting, flicking your hands periodically to ensure this unwanted residue is well clear of your aura. If you wish, a partner may perform this act of cleansing for you.

As a prelude to the actual exercise, the words of Bernard Shannon, author of *Immortalism in a Temporal World*, are worth recalling . . .

The aspirant must become aware of other-being while in the physical condition, and hold back part of himself from the maelstrom of human existence. To become so aware does not need deep study or meditation. Simply think of a greater area of being, without becoming too much concerned with what that area is like. Pure thought-energy without atomic constructions will be a sufficient interpretation ... Just *see* the higher area in the mind's eye; be aware that the area is there, without thinking or ruminating upon it. The mental picture must exist ...

Now you are ready for the exercise itself which, though capable of facilitating exploration of any interlife or past life, will be directed at the most recent between-life period. Should you prefer to examine another incarnation or discarnate existence, amend the exercise accordingly by asking to view that existence instead of the most recent *bardo* experience ...

Lie down, breathe deeply several times, and travel gently into a state of relaxation. If the exercise is being read to you, close your eyes, and relish the state of being relaxed, of listening to the pronunciation of each word. If reading the exercise yourself, proceed slowly, allowing a peaceful state of mind to overwhelm you before taking the first step towards the celestial sanctum. Either way, travel deep within yourself, focusing solely on going further and further into an altered state of reality. You are aware of nothing except your own mind and these words as they slip into your consciousness ...

Now visualize high in the sky, far beyond the clouds, a great cathedral, far grander and of far greater dimension than any place of worship that could possibly be constructed here on Earth. This celestial sanctum has a colossal double doorway placed squarely beneath huge arches and twin spires. A massive set of stone steps leads up to this entrance ... Concentrate on bringing this vast cathedral into being in every minute detail of its elaborate masonry and then see yourself alone, poised at the foot of the steps, looking up expectantly at the doorway ...

Start climbing the steps; notice the rough hewn granite as your shoes touch one step after another ... It's a long climb, but at last you reach the top and stand beneath the immensity of the wooden doors. Breathe deeply, pause, and then stretch out a hand to feel the texture of the wood, rubbing your hand lightly over the varnished surface stippled with knots and joins and cracks. Now give a slight push to one of the doors. It opens invitingly and, gradually, the dimly lit interior is revealed as the great hinges swing back and you step across the threshold onto the echoing flagstones of the vestibule.

Stand there and look around you; observe the high, vaulted ceilings, the stained glass windows, the massive columns, and row upon row of benches. Shafts of light fall diagonally across these benches, the air smells sweetly of incense, and you are overwhelmed by the solemnity, the stillness and the magnificence of the scene. But rather than proceed down the main aisle of the nave towards the altar, you turn instead to your left and walk towards the far wall. It's a long way away. As you advance you are aware that the flagstones beneath your feet have given way to polished marble and that the wall is panelled in dark hardwoods from floor to ceiling. Now, look along that wall for a door, a small door. It is not easy to see; you must look carefully. But at last you observe a small, brass doorhandle and you proceed towards it. When you arrive, open that door ...

When you walk through the doorway, you see a stone

stairway. The steps are narrow and well worn, and they lead down to the cellars. Move down these steps; feel yourself descending deeper and deeper into the very foundations of the cathedral. At the foot of the steps stands a man, an old man. His hair is white and he is wearing a long, black gown that reaches almost to his ankles. He is the guardian of the records and he is expecting you, but he wants to know why you are here. Explain your quest for self-exploration and ask to see the record of your last interlife. The old man, bowing his head, listens attentively to your explanation and grants your request . . .

Next, the guardian beckons you to follow him into the library. You seem to float behind the flapping tails of his gown as he sets off through the seemingly endless corridors, past shelf after shelf piled high with books. At last he comes to a halt between parallel lines of stacked volumes. He stands there for a few moments before pointing to a particular shelf of books. You follow the line of his arm, and your gaze alights upon your own name inscribed on the shelf in gold, embossed lettering. Read this name and verify that it is, indeed, the name by which you are known. Then survey the books that are on your shelf . . .

There are many, many books on this shelf of yours: one for each of your past lives and one for each of your interlives. Observe the succession of leather spines placed in chronological order from left to right. As this life is not yet over and its record has not yet been completed, the book located on the extreme right-hand side is that which contains full details of your most recent between-life experience. Ask the guardian for this record and watch him steadily as he reaches up, retrieves the book, and hands it to you. Hold the volume firmly, feeling the texture of its soft leather cover, and know that in a few moments you will open its pages to observe the contents of your last discarnate existence.

You may choose to look at any aspect of the interlife ... the threshold, the judgement board, planning the next life ... anything you wish. When you open the book (remember, a photograph album or videotape cassette may be retrieved in place of the book), you will do so with no fear. What is contained therein has already happened; it presents no surprises to your subconscious. You are merely looking at the record.

Now, open the book and examine whatever section of the interlife you have chosen to explore. Absorb the record calmly, passively, without emotion. You have all the time you wish.

When you have seen all there is to see, close the book and hand it back to the guardian who is waiting patiently some distance away. He replaces the book on its shelf and then motions for you to follow him once more through the labyrinthine library to the stairway leading back to the cathedral. You hasten after the old man until you are brought to the place where you first met. There, you bid him farewell for the time being and ascend the stairs, proceeding through the small door into the silence and majesty of the nave. You close the door behind you and pause for a while under the ornate ceilings before returning to the vestibule and the enormous doorway. Now you step outside the celestial sanctum and slowly descend the stone steps. And as you move one foot before the other you find that normal consciousness is slowly returning so that by the time you reach the foot of the staircase you are once more fully aware of your surroundings ...

Some people find that they become aware of their interlife memories upon following the guided visualization for the first time. But most people need to repeat the exercise several times before recall is coaxed into consciousness. Those who are most persistent – or who, like Heather Whiteholme in Chapter 8, are 'natural' visualizers – will find their efforts are rewarded with a stream of images. Often, insights will appear later in dreams or will register as intuitive flashes that intrude upon the everyday waking state.

As some of Dr Whitton's subjects have found during hypnosis, information may be withheld by the subconscious mind; blank pages might confront the inner eye when the book of the interlife is opened, for example. But anyone who encounters such resistance will understand intuitively that there may be a valid reason for this damming of the flow of memory. Incidentally, interlife memory can be enhanced by keeping a diary of dreams and personal intuitions. If this diary can be sustained while successive visits are made to the celestial sanctum, knowledge of the soul's interlives and past lives should be uncovered as surely and as steadily as a buried city reveals itself to the excavations of archaeologists.

14

The Meaning of the Interim

> 'Anything which throws light upon the
> Universe, anything which reveals us
> to ourselves, should be welcome in
> this world of riddles.'
>
> *Aleister Crowley, Magick*

Through self-revelation, the life between life places physical being in its proper perspective. Metaconsciousness tells us, above all, that the subtle and the spiritual in man – our essence – is beyond destruction. At death we leave behind our chosen vehicle of flesh and bones so that another stage of life may begin. The next world, being our natural home, brings awakening and remembrance and the restoration of clarity. And in seeing ourselves as we truly are, we are able to learn from the last expedition into earthly reality, assess our progress, and eventually plan the next incarnation according to our needs.

If all the world's a stage, the *bardo* is life in the

wings where the props, pulleys, prompt cards and all else that makes a theatrical production possible have been brought together ready for use. Well-performed or shoddily executed, the 'performance' of life incarnate goes on once the decision making, rehearsing and preparatory work have taken place. Each script is written, directed and produced by the performer, many scripts being required for the acting out of many lifetimes. Only through a relentless succession of exits and entrances can learning and growth be achieved.

Carefully or haphazardly, we choose our earthly circumstances. The message of metaconsciousness is that the life situation of every human being – whether a victim of AIDS, an aborted child, a movie star, a legless newspaper vendor or the President of the United States – is neither random nor inappropriate. Seen objectively from the interlife, every human experience is simply another lesson in the cosmic classroom. The more we learn from each lesson, the faster we evolve. Opportunities to love and serve are always sought in interlife planning and, consequently, they must be seen as fundamental to self-development. As restful and rejuvenating as the experience of solitude might be from time to time, karmic unfoldment demands human interaction.

Human existence only becomes comprehensible when the tiny segment between birth and death – our current reality – is placed in a cosmic context. No longer just a name given to a religious concept which may or may not have validity, life eternal is suddenly a reality and the overriding meaning and purpose of existence become dazzlingly clear, if difficult to convey in language. The interlife panor-

ama is breathtaking to behold: no space, no time . . .
awesome infinity forever.

All our lives and interlives lie within that infinity,
as do the karmic patterns which shape personal evolutionary development. And just as the most microscopic detail of our past-life actions and interlife
experience is open to inspection from this state, so
are we granted an overview of the journey thus far
. . . the unspeakably long odyssey that weaves in and
out of incarnation. Awareness of this greater reality
subjects earthbound values, attitudes and preoccu-
pations to rigorous revision by revealing that death
is merely a transition. Conscious immortality cannot
help but lead to personal reformation. As Carl Jung
wrote in *Memories, Dreams, Reflections*: '. . . Only
if we know that the thing which truly matters is
the infinite can we avoid fixing our interest upon
futilities.'

The testimony of Dr Whitton's subjects takes us
only so far. Becoming aware of guides, the board of
judgement, the planning process and other elements
of the interlife is the first step. Next we must seek
a fuller understanding of their respective functions
and their influence on incarnate existence. As the
learning proceeds, the prevailing rationalist-
materialistic orthodoxy of medical science must be
prepared to acknowledge a fresh dimension. One of
America's leading physicians, Dr Stanley R. Dean,
coined the term 'metapsychiatry' for the integration
of this dimension into established psychiatric practice. In *Psychiatry and Mysticism*, he states, 'Metapsychiatry is strongly interdisciplinary, having
synergistic relationships with parapsychology,
philosophy, religion and empirical logic. These

mutually supportive components can produce results that none can produce alone.'

For too long the healing of bodies and the healing of minds have been considered separate disciplines. The emergence of past-life therapy, however, indicates that the holistic approach will again be granted the status it once enjoyed. In his book *The Psyche in Medicine*, English psychiatrist Dr Arthur Guirdham perceived that . . .

> . . . cosmic factors in medicine will be more generally recognized as man's present increasing degree of psychic awareness is accentuated . . . Current medicine has turned its back on wisdom as the latter term was understood by the great sages and philosophers, who saw things not from a so-called scientific or religious aspect but as a whole. All one asks is that we accept that the inevitable truths of existence be permitted to lighten the shady colonnades of contemporary medicine.

Because the heartbeat of the soul is to be found in the interlife, there is every reason to suppose that metaconsciousness can open the healing arts and other disciplines to deeper levels of understanding. As more and more people make contact with their innermost selves and feel the harmony with universal order that characterizes the discarnate state, psychotherapy stands to make a major breakthrough. Just to know that this other reality exists can be life-changing in itself – reassuringly so. Holding these guarantees of absolute security we should be less inclined to falter or fear within the boundaries of incarnate life. If we do, the fault lies in our inability to maintain visions of truth while grappling with earthbound reality.

Most importantly, knowledge of the interlife intensifies personal responsibility. If we accept that the Earth plane is where between-life intentions are put to the test, daily life becomes charged with new meaning and purpose. And no matter how difficult earthly circumstances may be, a loving source awaits to engulf every human being in beauty and grandeur at the close of each brief existence. The *bardo* is where we belong, planet Earth being no more than a very necessary testing ground conducive to spiritual evolution.

Although much has been accomplished, the life between lives is an untapped human resource which remains in a preliminary stage of understanding. Only massive research can hope to reveal the deeper secrets of this other world and its potential for human advancement. This book is a record of initial explorations. As scientists penetrate further into the interlife, a greater understanding of our discarnate heritage will surely emerge. The study of metaconsciousness, with its capacity for breaking down the barriers of birth and death, can hardly be invested with greater relevance to the human condition. It compels us to understand why we are here and what we must do.

Bibliography

BOOKS

ALLEN, T. G., translator, *The Book of the Dead.*
Chicago: University of Chicago Press, 1974.

BENDIT, L. J., *The Mirror of Life*. Wheaton, Illinois:
Theosophical Publishing House, 1967.

BERNARD, R., *Messages from the Celestial
Sanctum*. San Jose: Rosicrucian Press, 1980.

BERNSTEIN, MOREY, *The Search for Bridey
Murphy*. New York: Pocket Books, 1978.

BLAVATSKY, H. P., *The Secret Doctrine*. Pasadena,
Ca., Theosophical University Press, 1952.

BOEHME, J. *The Signature of All Things*.
Cambridge: James Clarke and Company, 1969.

BROWN, MICHAEL H., *PK, A Report on the Power.
of Psychokinesis*. Blauvelt, New York:
Steinerbooks, 1976.

BRUNTON, PAUL, *The Quest of the Overself*.
Philadelphia: The Blakiston Company, 1938.

BUCKE, RICHARD MAURICE, MD, *Cosmic
Consciousness*. New York: E. P. Dutton and
Co, 1967.

CHENEY, S., *Men Who Have Walked with God*.
New York: Alfred A. Knopf, 1968.

CHRISTIE-MURRAY, DAVID, *Reincarnation:
Ancient Beliefs and Modern Evidence*.
Newton Abbot, Devon: David and Charles,
1981.

CRABTREE, ADAM, *Multiple Man*. Toronto: William Collins Sons, 1985.

CURRIE IAN, *You Cannot Die*. Toronto: Methuen Publications, 1978.

DEAN, STANLEY R. (ed.), *Psychiatry and Mysticism*. Chicago: Nelson Hall, 1979.

DESCARTES, RENÉ, *Discourse on Method*. (Ed. and translator, L. Fafleur). New York: Library of Liberal Arts, 1960.

DETHLEFSEN, THORWALD, *Voices from Other Lives*. New York: M. Evans and Co., 1977.

EASTON, STEWART C., *Man and World in the Light of Anthroposophy*. New York: The Anthroposophic Press, 1975.

EVANS-WENTZ, W. Y., *The Tibetan Book of the Dead*. London: Oxford University Press, 1960.

FIORE, DR EDITH, *You Have Been Here Before*. New York: Coward, McCann and Geoghegan, 1978.

FISHER, JOE, *The Case For Reincarnation*. Toronto: William Collins Sons, 1984. London: Granada Publishing, 1985.

FISHER, JOE, with PETER COMMINS, *Predictions*. Toronto: William Collins Sons, 1980.

FORTUNE, D., *The Esoteric Orders and Their Work*. Minnesota: Llewellyn Publications, 1971.

FRAZER, SIR JAMES GEORGE, *The Belief in Immortality*. London: Dawsons of Pall Mall, 1968.

FREEMANTLE, FRANCESCA and TRUNGPA, CHOGYAM, *The Tibetan Book of the Dead*. Chicago: University of Chicago Press, 1974.

GALLUP, DR GEORGE, Jr. with WILLIAM PROCTOR, *Adventures in Immortality*. New York: McGraw Hill, 1982.

GRAY, LOUIS HERBERT, (ed.), *The Mythology of All Races*. Boston: Marshall Jones, 1918.

GUIRDHAM, ARTHUR, *The Psyche in Medicine*. Jersey: Neville Spearman, 1978.

HALL, MANLY P., *The Secret Teachings of All Ages*. Los Angeles: The Philosophical Research Society, 1928.

———, *Reincarnation: The Cycle of Necessity*. Los Angeles: The Philosophical Research Society, 1978.

———, *Death to Rebirth*. Los Angeles: The Philosophical Research Society, 1979.

HAPPOLD, F. C., *Mysticism*. London: Penguin, 1963.

HEAD, JOSEPH, and CRANSTON, S. L., (eds.), *Reincarnation: The Phoenix Fire Mystery*. New York: Crown Publishers, 1977.

HEINDEL, M., *The Rosicrucian Cosmo-Conception*. San Jose: Rosicrucian Fellowship, 1911.

HOLMES, C. P., *Man's Psychological Illusions: Adventures in Psychology and Mysticism*. (Lecture notes, privately published.) Toronto: York University, 1984.

HOWE, QUINCY Jr., *Reincarnation for the Christian*. Philadelphia: The Westminster Press, 1974.

HUMPHREYS, CHRISTMAS, *Karma and Rebirth*. London: John Murray, 1943.

IVERSON, JEFFREY, *More Lives Than One?* London: Pan Books, 1977.

JOHNSON, J., *The Path of the Masters*. India: Radha Soami Satsang Beas, 1939.

JUNG, CARL, *Memories, Dreams, Reflections*.

(Edited and transcribed by Aniela Jaffé;
translated by Richard and Clara Winston.)
London: Collins and Routledge and Kegan Paul,
1963.

——, *Mysterium Coniunctionis*. (Translated by
R. F. C. Hull.) Princeton: Princeton University
Press, Bollingen Series, Vol. 14, 1963.

KARDEC, ALLEN, *Book on Mediums*. Boston:
Colby and Rich, 1874.

KUESHANA, E., *The Ultimate Frontier*. Chicago:
The Stelle Group, 1963.

LANGDON-DAVIES, JOHN, *Man: Known and
Unknown*. London: Secker and Warburg,
1960.

LANGLEY, NOEL, *Edgar Cayce on Reincarnation*.
London: Howard Baker, 1969.

LE GOFF, JACQUES, *The Birth of Purgatory*.
Chicago: University of Chicago Press, 1984.

LEVI, ELIPHAS, *Transcendental Magic*.
(Translated by A. E. Waite.) London: Rider and
Company, 1896.

LEWIS, H. SPENCER, *Rosicrucian Manual*. San
Jose: Rosicrucian Press, 1918.

——, *Mansions of the Soul*. San Jose: Rosicrucian
Press, 1975.

MACREADY, ROBERT, *The Reincarnations of
Robert Macready*. New York: Zebra, 1980.

MANNING, MATTHEW, *The Link*. Gerrards Cross:
Colin Smythe, 1974.

MOODY, RAYMOND A., Jr., *Life After Life*. New
York: Bantam Books, 1981.

MOORE, MARCIA and DOUGLAS, MARK,
Reincarnation: Key to Immortality. York Cliffs:
Arcane Publications, 1968.

MOSS, PETER with KEETON, JOE, *Encounters with the Past.* New York: Penguin, 1981.

MULLER, MAX, (ed.), *The Sacred Books of the East.* Vols. 1–49. London: Oxford University Press, 1880–1904.

NETHERTON, MORRIS and SCHIFFRIN, NANCY, *Past Lives Therapy.* New York: William Morrow, 1978.

OUSPENSKY, P. D., *Tertium Organum.* New York: Alfred A. Knopf, 1959.

OWEN, A. R., GEORGE, *Psychic Mysteries of Canada.* Toronto: Fitzhenry and Whiteside, 1975, pp. 208–18.

———, *Can We Explain the Poltergeist?* New York: Helix, 1963.

PAGELS, E., *The Gnostic Gospels.* New York: Random House, 1979.

PERCIVAL, H.W., *Thinking and Destiny.* New York: The Word Foundation, 1946.

PERKINS, JAMES S., *Through Death to Rebirth* Wheaton, Theosophical Publishing House, 1982.

Qabbalah Literature. The Sepher Ha-Zohar. The Sepher Yetzirah. The Sepher Sephiroth.

RAPHAEL, A., *Goethe and The Philosopher's Stone.* New York: Garrett, 1965.

RAWLINGS, DR MAURICE, *Beyond Death's Door.* London: Sheldon Press, 1983.

RING, KENNETH, *Life at Death.* New York: Coward, McCann and Geoghegan, 1980.

ROBERTS, JANE, *The Seth Material.* New York: Bantam Books, 1981.

SABOM, MICHAEL B., MD, *Recollections of Death.* London: Corgi Books, 1982.

SHANNON, BERNARD, *Immortalism in a Temporal World*. London: Vision Press, 1974.

SILBERER, H., *Hidden Symbolism of Alchemy and the Occult Arts*. New York: Dover, 1917.

SINGH, K., *The Wheel of Life*. Delhi, India: Ruhani Satsang, 1965.

——, *The Mystery of Death*. Delhi: Ruhani Satsang, 1968

STEINER, RUDOLF, *An Outline of Occult Science*. Spring Valley, N.Y.: Anthroposophic Press, 1939.

——, *Between Death and Rebirth*. London: Rudolf Steiner Press, 1975.

——, *Reincarnation and Karma*. London: Rudolf Steiner Press, 1977.

——, *Investigations into Life Between Death and Rebirth*. Lectures *1*, *2*. Milan: October 26, 27, 1912.

STEVENSON, DR IAN, *Cases of the Reincarnation Type (Vols. 1–4)*. Charlottesville: University Press of Virginia, 1975–83.

——, *Twenty Cases Suggestive of Reincarnation*. Charlottesville: University Press of Virginia, 1974.

STRONG, A. H., *Systematic Theology*. Chicago: The Judson Press, 1907.

SUGRUE, THOMAS, *There Is a River*. New York: Dell, 1961.

TOYNBEE, ARNOLD and others, *Man's Concern with Death*. London: Hodder and Stoughton, 1968.

TRINE, RALPH WALDO, *In Tune with the Infinite*. London: G. Bell and Sons, 1947.

WALKER, E. D., *Reincarnation: A Study of*

Forgotten Truth. New York: Theosophical
Publishing Co., 1904.
WAMBACH, HELEN, *Life Before Life*. New York:
Bantam Books, 1979.
WATTS, ALAN, *The Supreme Identity*. New York:
Pantheon Books, 1972.
WEED, JOSEPH J., *Wisdom of the Mystic Masters*.
New York: Parker Publishing, 1968.

BOOKLETS AND RESEARCH PAPERS

DEAN, CHARLES DANA, FRC, *The Celestial
Sanctum: Its Origin, Purposes and Program of
Services*. San Jose: The Rosicrucian Press, 1975.
STEVENSON, IAN, 'Research into Man's Survival
After Death'. *Journal of Nervous and Mental
Disease*, Vol. 165, pp. 152–70, 1977.
———, 'American Children Who Claim to
Remember Past Lives'. *Journal of Nervous and
Mental Disease*, Vol. 171, pp. 742–48, 1983.
WHITTON, JOEL L., 'Hypnotic Time Regression
and Reincarnation Memories'. *New Horizons*,
June 1976.
———, 'Karma in Reincarnation'. The Rosicrucian
Digest, October 1978.
———, 'Xenoglossia: A Subject with Two Possible
Instances'. *New Horizons*, September 1978.
———, 'Belief Systems and Reincarnation'. In
Applied Systems and Cybernetics, Vol. 2,
edited by G. E. Lasker, New York: Pergamon,
1980.

Index

The best in occult and astrology – now available in Grafton Books

Harrison Ainsworth
Lancashire Witches   £2.50 ☐

Colin Wilson
The Occult   £4.95 ☐
Mysteries   £5.95 ☐
Starseekers   £1.95 ☐

Michael Bentine
The Door Marked Summer   £1.95 ☐

Terence Whitaker
Lancashire's Ghosts and Legends (illustrated)   £1.50 ☐
Yorkshire's Ghosts and Legends (illustrated)   £1.50 ☐

Erica Jong
Witches   £5.95 ☐

Henry C Roberts (Editor and translator)
The Complete Prophecies of Nostradamus   £2.50 ☐

Stearn Robinson and Tom Corbett
The Dreamer's Dictionary   £2.95 ☐

Doris Collins
A Woman of Spirit   £2.50 ☐

Graham Philips and Martin Keatman
The Green Stone (illustrated)   £2.50 ☐

To order direct from the publisher just tick the titles you want
and fill in the order form.   **GOA182**

Modern society – now available in Grafton Books

To order direct from the publisher just tick the titles you want and fill in the order form.

Famous personalities you've always wanted to read about – now available in Grafton Books

Dirk Bogarde
A Postillion Struck by Lightning (illustrated)   £2.50 ☐
Snakes and Ladders (illustrated)   £2.95 ☐
An Orderly Man (illustrated)   £2.95 ☐

Muhammad Ali with Richard Durham
The Greatest: My Own Story   £1.95 ☐

Fred Lawrence Guiles
Norma Jean (illustrated)   £3.95 ☐

Becky Yancey
My Life with Elvis   £1.95 ☐

Shelley Winters
Shelley   £1.95 ☐

Stewart Granger
Sparks Fly Upward   £1.95 ☐

Billie Jean King
Billie Jean King (illustrated)   £1.95 ☐

Stephen Davies
Bob Marley (illustrated)   £2.95 ☐

Pat Jennings
An Autobiography (illustrated)   £1.95 ☐

Ann Morrow
The Queen (illustrated)   £2.50 ☐
The Queen Mother (illustrated)   £2.95 ☐

Pat Phoenix
Love, Curiosity, Freckles & Doubt (illustrated)   £1.95 ☐
All My Burning Bridges (illustrated)   £1.95 ☐

To order direct from the publisher just tick the titles you want
and fill in the order form.   **GM581**

Books of historical interest now available in
Grafton Books

David Daiches
Edinburgh (illustrated)   £1.95   ☐
Glasgow (illustrated)   £3.95   ☐

Paul Johnson
The National Trust Book of British Castles (illustrated)   £4.95   ☐

Nigel Nicolson
The National Trust Book of Great Houses (illustrated)   £4.95   ☐

Frank Delaney
James Joyce's Odyssey (illustrated)   £2.95   ☐

Stan Gébler Davies
James Joyce: A Portrait of the Artist (illustrated)   £2.50   ☐

To order direct from the publisher just tick the titles you want
and fill in the order form.

GM681

History – now available in Grafton Books

Frederick Engels
The Condition of the Working Class in England £1.95 ☐

Field Marshal Lord Carver
The Seven Ages of the British Army (illustrated) £4.95 ☐

Christopher Farman
The General Strike (illustrated) £1.95 ☐

Sir Arthur Bryant
Samuel Pepys: The Man in the Making £3.95 ☐
Samuel Pepys: The Years of Peril £3.95 ☐
Samuel Pepys: Saviour of the Navy £3.95 ☐

Larry Collins and Dominique Lapierre
Freedom at Midnight (illustrated) £3.95 ☐
O Jerusalem (illustrated) £3.95 ☐

Angus Calder
The People's War (illustrated) £3.95 ☐

Thomas Pakenham
The Year of Liberty £1.95 ☐

Antony Bridge
The Crusaders (illustrated) £3.95 ☐

Joyce Marlow
The Tolpuddle Martyrs (illustrated) £2.95 ☐

John Erickson
The Road to Stalingrad (illustrated) £6.95 ☐
The Road to Berlin £8.95 ☐

Robert Fisk
In Time of War (illustrated) £4.95 ☐

To order direct from the publisher just tick the titles you want
and fill in the order form.

All these books are available at your local bookshop or newsagent, or can be ordered direct from the publisher.

To order direct from the publishers just tick the titles you want and fill in the form below.

Name _____

Address _____

_____

Send to:
Grafton Cash Sales
PO Box 11, Falmouth, Cornwall TR10 9EN.

Please enclose remittance to the value of the cover price plus:

UK 60p for the first book, 25p for the second book plus 15p per copy for each additional book ordered to a maximum charge of £1.90.

BFPO 60p for the first book, 25p for the second book plus 15p per copy for the next 7 books, thereafter 9p per book.

Overseas including Eire £1.25 for the first book, 75p for second book and 28p for each additional book.

_____

Grafton Books reserve the right to show new retail prices on covers, which may differ from those previously advertised in the text or elsewhere.